UA Training Technologies: 4

Using Role Plays in Human Resource Development

Using Role Plays in Human Resource Development

J. William Pfeiffer, Ph.D., J.D.

Arlette C. Ballew

University Associates, Inc.
8517 Production Avenue
San Diego, California 92121

Table of Contents

Introduction

This is the fourth book in the University Associates Training Technologies collection. The first three discussed the use of structured experiences; instruments; and lecturettes, theory, and models in human resorce development. These technologies, and role playing as well, all involve "learning by doing" or "experiential learning." Although there may well be cognitive input involved in all of them, it is balanced by the direct learner involvement that has been shown to be necessary for optimum transfer of learning in adults.

There are a number of different ways of changing people's attitudes and of developing individuals' behavioral skills. Structured experiences stress high participation and "processing" of data generated during interactive activities. The use of paper-and-pencil instruments involves learners in self-assessment and direct feedback. The didactic component comes from the theory underlying the items of the scale. The experiential lecture is more involving than the traditional lecture approach because it incorporates activities on the part of the audience. These interactions are designed to personalize the points of the lecturette and/or to generate readiness for the next topic.

Discussion also is a time-honored teaching intervention that has been extended and refined in participation training. The case-study and gaming methods, in which situations are acted out to some degree, are closely related to role playing. The fifth book in the Training Technologies collection is on the use of case studies, simulations, and games in human resource development.

Role playing, the subject of this book, allows the participants an opportunity to "try on" and/or practice new behaviors in a relatively safe environment. Participants can see, practice, and receive coaching on such interpersonal skills as active listening, interviewing, problem solving, communicating, information sharing, and risk taking. Group members can exchange roles in order to experience multiple sides of a situation. They can assess the effectiveness of various approaches and can provide feedback to one another on their styles of interacting. Furthermore, role playing can be used to work through issues or problems that arise in real life but which are difficult to examine objectively.

Shaw, Corsini, Blake, and Mouton (1980) identify four types of role playing: theatrical, sociological, dissimulative, and educational. This book is limited to role playing for educational (training and development) purposes. It presents a clear description of the advantages and potential disadvantages of this technology and a practical strategy for the effective use of role plays in experiential training designs.

A Background for Using Role Plays in Human Resource Development

The History of Role Playing

The technique of role playing is an outgrowth of the age-old idea of practice or rehearsal and was reinforced by the development in this century of the case-study method for teaching. Role playing in its modern form was first used by J.L. Moreno, a Viennese psychiatrist, in working with mentally disturbed patients (Moreno, 1923, 1953). He called it "psychodrama," and his purpose was to give the patient insight into some of his or her relationships with others by having the patient play the role of these other persons. (Psychodrama, or therapeutic role playing, is still used in counseling and therapy today.) Moreno saw role playing as an opportunity for an individual to shed the inhibitions and restrictions imposed by society and by the fear of criticism, punishment, or ridicule. He maintained that this reduction of inhibition is necessary before the individual can employ the creativity and spontaneity that are necessary for learning and change to occur. Then the opportunity to experience new feelings and practice new behaviors helps to stabilize the new, desired behavior.

In 1933, a German military psychologist named Simoneit devised a number of action procedures very similar to current role-playing techniques by which officers in the German army could estimate the qualities of army recruits. In the 1940s and 1950s, the U.S. Office of Strategic Services Assessment Staff used role playing in the selection of people for secret wartime work, and the British army employed similar procedures in its officer-selection program. Role playing began to be used in the United States for training purposes during World War II, and its use in industrial training was reported by Lippitt (1943) and French (1945), followed by Argyris (1951), Maier (1952, 1953, 1973), Corsini (1957, 1966), Starr (1977), and many others. Today it is an accepted part of the trainer's repertoire.

What a Role Play Is and What It Is Not

Role playing is a technique in which people are presented with roles in the form of a case or scenario, then act out the roles in order to experience them for educational purposes. The ways in which these roles were approached by the role players then is discussed, and the action may or may not be tried again. Role playing is, then, a spontaneous human interaction that involves realistic behavior under artificial or "imagined" conditions.

Role playing generally is used for one of several reasons:

1. To *practice behavior in preparation* for a new role or an anticipated problem situation;
2. To *examine a problem situation or past incident* in order to learn how it could be/have been handled better;
3. To *create insight* into the motivations and roles of others or oneself.

In role playing, the emphasis is on developing new skills and insights and on solving and preventing problems. This differs from the lecture and the textbook approaches to learning, in which the emphasis may be on principles and determining the "right" answer.

With a real-life situation, one may never be sure that it was handled in the best way. The role play is a type of simulation in which a person or group can be introduced repeatedly to the same situation and can measure the effects of various behaviors. Because the situation can be repeated with various approaches, the impact of those various approaches can be assessed and discussed.

Role playing is distinguished from another major educational approach, the case study, primarily in terms of focus and impact.

The case study is more likely to be centered primarily on cognitive learning, whereas a role play typically emphasizes both cognitive and affective development on the part of learners. For example, in a case study the group might decide that person A should apologize to person B. That would be the result of the group's work on the subject. In a role play, however, A would actually go to B and apologize. Both A and B would say how that felt and whether it worked for them; they might retry it with A modifying his or her apology and/or B modifying his or her response. Thus, role playing demonstrates the difference between *thinking* and *doing*. Because the case study has a there-and-then content emphasis it creates considerably less learner involvement than the role play and less potential for promoting transferable learning that is "owned" by the participants.

A Rationale for Using Role Plays

A human being thinks, acts, and feels at the same time, but the three processes may not be congruent. The most effective way to communicate with or teach a person is to reach the totality, the thinking, feeling, and behaving parts of the individual. Experience in the training and development field has made it clear that learning the principles of human behavior has little value uness it is supplemented by affective understanding and skill practice. The best kind of practice is performing under competent supervision in an atmosphere that is free of serious risk to oneself or others. Role playing offers an opportunity to practice one's human relations skills in a lifelike setting, to experiment and try out new behaviors without running the risks that such experimentation entails in real life. The repetition that is part of many role-play designs sharpens and reinforces the new insights, feelings, and behavioral skills. In addition, a properly planned role-play activity involves discussion and analysis of crucial issues.

The participants in a role play engage in actual behavior, confronting problems and other people. They receive immediate information about the effects of their behavior and about how they could act differently. Thus, they can relate the feedback to their actual ways of behaving in specific situations. This creates the motivation to inquire and to experiment with new behaviors.

Because role playing is an *active* technique, the participant in a role play gains many insights while *in* a role that would not occur in clinical reading or discussion of a situation. There is no separation between thoughts, words, and action. Role playing provides a chance to fully experience a situation, including "the other side," whether that be, for example, a boss/subordinate, husband/wife, parent/child, or union/managment situation or an intercultural experience. This allows the learnings to become internalized, which does not occur from merely reading about something. In fact, during a role play, participants often make the mistakes for which they have been criticizing others, especially their managers, spouses, or co-workers.

The discussion that follows the role play is the core of the learning experience. It typically reveals various attitudes and habits that can be clarified, evaluated, and modified through group interaction. Observers can note not only what occurs in the role play but also their own reactions. The comments of all role players and observers about more effective ways to deal with the situation can be explored, and the situation can be reenacted to test the new ideas. For these reasons, role playing has a wide utility in leadership and management development, training in communication skills, improvement of interpersonal relationships, and team development.

Role playing is widely used by the military in war games, by assessment centers to determine the optimum career path of participants, and in assertion training to develop the skills and concepts needed for individuals to stand up for their rights in the face of potential conflict. Role playing lends itself particularly well to the exploration of ideas and theories in interpersonal communication and leadership roles. Perhaps the most widespread use of role playing in training and development has been in courses and workshops in communication skills and leadership development. It also has been used frequently to teach interviewing skills, to both interviewers and potential interviewees.

The unique values of role playing include the following:

- It requires the person to *carry out* a thought or decision. As stated above, it demonstrates the difference between thinking and doing.

- It permits *practice* in carrying out an action and allows people "another shot" at it.
- It makes clear the fact that good human relations require *skill* in the same sense that playing golf requires skill. Although many of us feel that we are expected to know how to solve interpersonal problems and deal with people merely because we are adults, the fact that problems, misunderstandings, counselors, and training exist is evidence that most of us do not have these skills inherently.
- It accomplishes *attitude changes* effectively by placing people in specified roles. This demonstrates that a person's behavior is not only a function of his or her personality but also of the *situation* in which he or she happens to be.
- It trains a person to be aware of and sensitive to the feelings of others. This awareness functions as feedback on the *effect* of one's behavior.
- It develops a fuller appreciation of the important part played by *feelings* in determining behavior in social situations.
- It enables people to *discover* their personal faults. For example, the person who enjoys making wisecracks may discover that they annoy or hurt others.
- It permits training in the *control of feelings and emotions.* For example, by repeatedly playing the role of a supervisor, a person can practice not becoming irritated by complaints.

In role playing, a person can learn not only how to act in different ways but also why other people may act as they do. This creates enormous potential for the improvement of interpersonal interactions.

Role-Play Objectives

Although role playing has been used effectively in counseling and therapy, we have chosen not to discuss that application in this book. In the field of human resource development, a number of objectives can be realized through role playing; these include training, communication, behavior rehearsal, behavior modeling, demonstration, and assessment and evaluation.

Training and Communication

One of the primary reasons for role playing is to provide training for skills in dealing with information or insights into the nature of human behavior. Role playing has the potential to generate affective content for the purposes of exploring relationships between feelings and behavior in human interactions. Role plays can be selected or devised to study the probable effects of different behaviors on the participants in a problem situation, thereby providing a potential learning opportunity for individuals to develop an increased sensitivity both to their own and to others' feelings. It also can be used to create a data base for interpersonal feedback within a workshop. Thus, role playing is suitable in training for any situation or job that involves human interaction.

Inasmuch as many experiential learning concepts are often difficult for participants to apply to their everyday work, role playing also offers a vehicle for delivering theory input in an engrossing and stimulating way that is relevant to real-world problem situations. Theoretical concepts can be incorporated into role descriptions and into the role-play problem.

The technology also can be used to help people to improve their communication skills through practice, feedback, and attempting to vary the presentation in order to make it more effective. This can be particularly useful in training not only managers but also medical practitioners, police and other public servants, parents, salespeople, educators, lawyers, and scientists. Thus, role playing is not limited to applications in which one is attempting to change attitudes and behaviors; it also is useful in creating insights and "polishing" interpersonal skills.

Behavior Rehearsal and Behavior Modeling

The operant conditioning or "stimulus-response" theory of behavior modification led to the introduction of programed instruction. Then it became clear that although programed instruction could increase an individual's knowledge, it could not provide the insight that comes from trying out new behavior in ongoing human situations. Role playing has become an integral part of the behaviorist's approach to learning because it provides opportunities for introducing new stimuli and evoking new responses; it provides opportunities for reinforcing desired behavior and diminishing undesired behavior; and it provides opportunities for learning by doing. The two most common applications of role playing in behavior modification are behavior rehearsal and behavior modeling.

In *behavior rehearsal* the individual is asked to deal with a specific problem that has been identified through small-group discussion, a problem census, a presentation, or the individual's own analysis of areas in which he or she wishes to practice and improve. The facilitator introduces ground rules or procedures as guidelines to use in coping with the situation under consideration (e.g., guidelines for dealing with angry customers, procedures for making a sales call). These also serve as criteria for determining whether the role player's behavior is appropriate and effective. The participants then identify a specific situation in this area that they want to deal with more effectively. The group is split into small "rehearsal" groups (three to eight members each), and a specific and repeatable rehearsal procedure is defined so that all participants have the opportunity to practice dealing with the problem situation. Multiple trys and a format for feedback are built into the process. If the training group is small, the format can be less formalized although still structured; that is, the facilitator can ask one or more group members to begin the role play as a demonstration, with other members offering suggestions.

Behavior modeling is based on the premise that people may handle a situation ineffectively because they do not know *how* to handle it, i.e., they do not have a model for dealing with it. In organizational settings, behavior modeling often is used to teach procedures for dealing with clients, customers, and subordinates. First the participants are presented with a procedural model; then they observe a *behavioral display* in the form of an enactment, film, or videotape. Group members then try out their own skills in dealing with the situation or issue, through either structured or unstructured role playing.

Demonstration

The role-play approach can be used to inform and instruct in almost every situation in which films, lectures, and demonstrations are suitable. A role play can demonstrate various skills and concepts in interpersonal relations and communications. It can be used to teach specific methods. It can be used to give the observers information about how a certain role should be filled. In such a case, the role play serves to "model" the behaviors desired; it is one type of audiovisual aid.

Assessment and Evaluation

Role playing is one of the best ways to provide evaluation of and feedback to people relative to increasing their effectiveness in various interpersonal situations. It can provide an impactful means of experiencing different behaviors in order to evaluate their effects.

Problems being focused on by a participant group can be "staged" to achieve a different perspective. Role playing also can be used for group diagnosis, to provide better understanding of the role players by seeing and hearing them in action. This would be particularly helpful in group problem solving or team building.

In addition, role playing has been applied to personnel selection and other types of job evaluation, as in assessment centers. The assessment center is an extension of the testing processes of both psychometrics and "situation testing," an outgrowth of Moreno's work that was developed by the military in the 1940s. Specific factors related to performance are identified and standardized, and the role-player's performance is evaluated by experts. It is important in this instance that the role-play situation and problem bear resemblance to real life and that they elicit behavior that is typical of the individual. In assessment centers, role playing is used for both assessment and demonstration. It usually is combined with instruments, simulations, interaction activities, and a variety of small-group tasks. This is most frequently applied to the selection and development of managers.

Role playing has an advantage over interviews, instruments, and diagnostic tests in that it is spontaneous, natural, and in the here-and-now. It provides the evaluators with direct experience that is not distorted by errors in communication; thus, it is more accurate for the prediction of human behavior (Borgatta, 1956).

The Advantages and Potential Disadvantages of Using Role Plays

Role playing has a number of obviously desirable applications; however, there also are some potential disadvantages. The facilitator needs to be aware of both in order to be able to optimize the benefits and to minimize the potentially negative aspects.

Advantages

Participants typically experience role playing as an *engaging* activity. Because almost everyone knows how to play someone else's role, participants tend to enjoy role plays, and it is unnecessary for them to learn new skills in order to benefit from the process. Also, role playing often is fun, although overplaying a part can detract from the learning. When role playing is conducted skillfully, the situations have a high credibility for participants, thereby reducing resistance to learning relevant skills and theory.

The technique is highly *flexible.* The facilitator can change the role play as it is being conducted, and the materials can be edited to fit particular situations. Role playing can be engaged in for brief or long periods. The technique often *reduces the threat* of interpersonal interaction: it sometimes is easier to explore oneself by projecting oneself into a role than to expose oneself directly. Participants are allowed to carry out decisions without the danger of embarrassing or incriminating themselves in "real" situations. Role playing can increase participants' awareness about the effects of feelings on social behavior.

Perhaps the most decided advantage of role playing in a training context is that it uses the experiences of participants in ways that *increase their ownership of learning.* As it provides a vehicle for focused feedback to individual participants, it can assist in developing the expression of feelings. Human problems in systems can be studied through the medium of role playing in a way that brings the "human factor" of organizational situations into sharper focus. Because it has the potential to *develop skills* in self-expression, listening, communicating points of view, and interpersonal interaction, role playing can raise participants' consciousness about the need for skills in human interaction. It also can permit the simulation of problem issues that arise infrequently in personal or work situations but are very important when they do arise. Thus, role playing offers participants the opportunity to gain hard-to-obtain experience in dealing with such situations. Because role playing frequently affects a participant's perception of a problem or situation, the new attitudes and behaviors tend to carry over to back-home situations.

Potential Disadvantages

Several potential disadvantages are inherent in the role-play technique. One obvious one is that the artificiality or superficiality of situations depicted in role-play scenarios can allow participants to discount the value of their learning because of the apparent over-simplification of the situation. Similarly, role playing can deteriorate into play, and the serious learning potential that is inherent in the process thereby can be jeopardized.

Participants often lose themselves in a role and engage in inadvertent self-disclosure, exposure, and ventilation. It is important that the facilitator point out this possibility to participants. The facilitator should be particularly aware of this disadvantage in order to avoid the ethical breach of allowing people unknowingly to make themselves vulnerable. Role playing can be a threatening experience for a significant minority of participants, and the facilitator needs to be sensitive to the pressures faced by participants.

Another disadvantage is that roles sometimes reinforce stereotypes and caricature people's behavior. This unfortunate side effect can be avoided if the facilitator ensures that role descriptions are credible and nonstereotypical and that role players are instructed not to caricature their roles.

A fifth problem arises when role plays are staged in front of an audience: the passivity of the audience can lessen the impact of the learning. In such a case, it is important that members of the audience have active roles as observers or coaches.

Sixth, role-playing situations can overpersonalize problem situations; for example,in team building, problems facing organizational work units sometimes are aggravated by a tendency to perceive feedback personally and to see issues in terms of individuals. Role playing can, through such overinvolvement, generate excess affect. The facilitator should be aware of the need to keep the learning focus sharply delineated.

2

Evaluating and Selecting Role Plays

Before considering role playing as a training technology, the facilitator must be clear about the goals of the session and must consider whether role playing is the best way to achieve them. Much of the training value of a role-play case depends on the scope of the generalizations that can be drawn from the results. For this reason, two important factors in screening a role play are the extent to which it typifies a broad range of problems in the area to be considered (management, personnel, intergroup, etc.) and the extent to which it illustrates and highlights the methods and principles for dealing with these problems. Another factor is the interest value of the role play and the challenge that it offers. A role play that lacks conflict and variety may be too boring to grab the interest of the participants. Of course, the overriding factor is the relationship of the role play to the overall training objectives, i.e., whether the activity will contribute to the goals of the session.

It is best if the facilitator has some knowledge of the group of participants (work team, department, organization, family, club, etc.) that will be attending the role-play session, as well as of the *norms, standards, and problems* that are present in the environment in which these people interact. A role play then can be selected to fit the needs, goals, interests, and expectations of the participants. If the participants are not members of an intact group, it will be up to the facilitator to select the best role play possible, given the backgrounds of the individual participants.

Appendix 1 of this book contains a list of role plays published in the University Associates series of *Handbooks* and *Annuals*.

Studying the actual role plays listed in the Appendix will provide an overview of the types of problems, situations, and structural interventions that can be found in good role plays.

Typical Problem Situations

In general, role playing in HRD is used to examine five typical kinds of problems:

1. Power and authority
2. Morale and cohesion
3. Goals and objectives
4. Norms and standards
5. Change and development

These areas of difficulty appear in both private and organizational life, but most HRD applications deal with on-the-job situations, so those will be the ones discussed here. The important thing for the facilitator is to discern *what the problem issue is* and to *select a role play that deals specifically with that issue.*

Power and Authority

The problems of power and authority are of particular difficulty in modern society. More and more people who *possess* power and authority do not know how to exercise them effectively, and those in our society who are *subject* to power and authority have trouble accepting that fact. If a person's attitude about power or authority in general is one of antagonism or threat, that person is less competent to deal objectively with those issues. Self-defeating cycles of behavior may result. Role playing can be an effective way to examine and deal with attitudes and behaviors that stem from these issues.

Rejection and Suppression

Rejection by a significant person who possesses power or authority can cause great difficulty for an individual. The authority figure or powerful person's objective may be to eliminate disagreement, re-establish control, or facilitate "progress," but the person affected feels suppressed and discounted. This often results in antagonism toward the authority figure or withdrawal of the subordinate individual. Worse, the subordinate may conclude that he or she has been found lacking or unworthy. All these feelings can lead to unhealthy, unproductive, and even self-destructive behavior.

Role plays that focus on power and authority relationships (boss/subordinate, parent/child, doctor/patient, instructor/student, minister/parishoner, etc.) are ideal for helping people to explore their own relationships and to examine their attitudes about exercising authority and their reactions to authority.

Morale and Cohesion

Morale and cohesion typify a "team" feeling or *esprit de corps,* in which individuals feel a sense of union and shared responsibility. When these feelings are high, the members of the group commit effort. When these feelings are low, people lack commitment and may be emotionally absent.

Role playing can help people who are experiencing low morale to identify what is causing their discouragement or depression. They can identify alternatives and practice strategies to overcome their negative feelings and the self-defeating behavior that often accompanies it, replacing them with a more positive orientation.

Another reason for low morale may be difficulties in relationships. Role playing can be used to identify aspects of a relationship that are causing difficulties and what each individual does to contribute to the problem.

Goals and Objectives

Goals and objectives give form and purpose to human endeavors. If, however, goals and objectives are not clear, individuals may be working at cross-purposes with themselves or with other members of their group. Role plays can be used in various ways to aid people in (a) clarifying their goals, (b) redefining their goals, (c) establishing goals when none are specified, and (d) restructuring their activities to make goal-oriented actions possible.

Norms and Standards

Norms and standards reflect the shared expectations of a group of people. When these expectations are accurate, each person can anticipate what the other people will do and can correlate his or her own efforts in order to bring about a productive outcome. If the norms and standards of a group are so informal or at so low a level as to block productive or creative efforts, role playing can be used to identify them and to demonstrate how they block group and individual accomplishment.

Another way in which norms and standards affect people is that, over time, people begin to expect things to be done in certain ways. When an attempt is made to institute change, resistance often is encountered. Some role plays are designed to explore attitudes about pre-existing norms and standards and their purposes, thus helping people to let go of outmoded norms and standards and replace them with shared expectations that are more appropriate to the circumstances. This type of role playing is particularly helpful to the consultant who is attempting to effect organizational change, and it can be used in change efforts other than those concerning norms and standards, as the following section explains.

Change and Development

Planned change provides the option to learn the dynamics of change, strategies for causing it, and the skills necessary for creating positive change. This approach differs from older patterns that rely on evolution, one-step-at-a-time processes, or the use of force and pressure to bring about change.

Role playing can be used to allow individuals to practice different behaviors. Thus, it is one of the best approaches for dealing with resistance to change. A sense of being *able* to do things differently or better often changes resistance and resentment to enthusiasm for change and development.

Using Organization-Based Scenarios

There is some question about whether role plays should be based on conditions *within* the organization or system in which the training is conducted. In general, this should be done only after a considerable amount of training has been done with *general* cases. When cases are based on company experiences and/or details are "close to home," there may be unfavorable results. These include:

1. People who know about the situation may disagree on the basic issues in the problem, leading to polarization within the participant group.
2. Irrelevant or historical facts often are introduced into the role play; these disrupt both the role play itself and the subsequent discussion.
3. Persons who were involved in the original situation often exhibit defensive behaviors.
4. Participants tend to concentrate on solutions rather than focusing on aspects of the problem or the process.
5. Organizational situations often have many causes, and the human-relations dimensions within them can be obscured by other factors. Role playing may oversimplify such situations and lead to misleading generalizations.

In setting up role-play situations, it is, therefore, best to use simulated problems before attempting to use real organizational problems. Once the group has become accustomed to role playing, has become familiar with the basic skill principles, and appreciates the constructive interaction that occurs in group discussion, organizational situations may be role played effectively. It is best, however, to use problems that have not been resolved, to avoid the betrayal of confidences and the perceived necessity of "saving face," and because the insights gained in role playing can be utilized in solving the

problem. When a group is ready to role play organizational problems, different members of the group should present their own case
data for the group's consideration.

Other Selection Considerations

Aside from the suitability of the role-play content, the selection of
a role play will be affected by several other limitations imposed by
the particular case. These include the following:

- *The number of people* required to play the roles;
- *The complexity of background and role instructions,*
  measured against the participants' familiarity with role playing and ability to deal with complex data;
- *The time required* for providing instructions, role playing,
  rerunning the role play, feedback, observer reports, and
  discussion;
- *The amount of space needed and/or the number and complexity of props* required;
- *The amount of threat and emotional affect* likely to be
  generated by the role play, measured against the participants'
  ability to handle and process it;
- *The amount and type of data* likely to be generated during
  the role play and the processing discussions, measured
  against both the participants' and facilitator's experience in
  giving and receiving feedback and in working through such
  data;
- *The possible reactions of nonparticipants within the system*
  to the fact that others are engaging in this type of training
  and their ability to deal with the responses and *changes* in-
  curred among the role-play participants.

A good role play reproduces the most significant conditions
of a real-life situation with a minimum of detail. People are
understandably nervous about engaging in a role play. It is ineffective to add to their concerns by giving them a lot of information
about the case background to absorb. If the role players need to
know "information" about the role-play "organization" or situation, this material should be printed so that they can refer to it as

they go along. Similarly, instructions about how to role play should be separate from the actual role instructions and should be dealt with *before the role instructions are handed out.* A role-play design that is too complicated or that requires too many props or too much preparation may create unnecessary problems.

If more than one role play is to be used in the training design, the sequence of cases should follow a developmental sequence of principles and skills. Each case can involve the use of partially new and increasingly complex abilities.

3

Designing Role Plays

In designing role plays, the potential disadvantages of the technique can be avoided through certain design considerations, choice of role-play problems, dimensions of role-play structure, careful development of materials, and detailed preparation.

Design Considerations

In creating role-play situations, there are a number of useful design considerations. Within the situation itself and the descriptions of the roles of individual players, it often is important that there be a broad range of human problems. Unless the role play is intended to demonstrate ineffective behavior, participants should be given an opportunity to behave effectively. This is particularly true if the major objective of the role play is to develop skills, in which case the emphasis should be on acknowledging and reinforcing the desired results.

In the role-play situation it is ideal to have conflict and variety. As is stated previously, it generally is desirable to avoid getting too close to actual, current organizational situations. Appendix 1 at the end of this book lists the role plays published in the University Associates series of *Handbooks* and *Annuals*. Referring to the texts of these role plays can provide examples of the design considerations discussed in this chapter.

Choice of Role-Play Problems

There are many types of problems that can be suggested for creating role-play situations. It is possible to focus on personal problem behaviors such as being unable to say no or being shy. Problems indigenous to leadership situations can be set up easily for role playing; boss-subordinate interactions lend themselves to exploration, and performance appraisal—a special type of boss-subordinate behavior—can be studied effectively. It is easy to establish role-play situations that simulate various aspects of staff meetings, such as the influence of hidden agendas on the conduct of the meeting. Integration problems, such as a "we-they" attitude, also can be studied effectively. Peer relationships between colleagues can be role played, too. Other types of organizational problems include increasing costs, budget meetings, organizational change and resistance, interdepartmental competition, and so on. A basic type of role play establishes a situation between two people in which one has a problem or message to deliver to the other, and the second person's role is to respond and deal with the first person. It is perhaps more ambitious but entirely possible to design role plays that explore any aspect of a functioning organization and/or several participants.

If feasible, role plays can be developed to meet specific organizational needs and goals. Through interviews or written surveys, managers and potential participants can be asked to suggest program objectives and to supply pertinent data. Analyses of current data and statements of training needs also will help to pinpoint critical issues. As has been suggested earlier, it probably is wise *not* to use an issue that currently is "hot," unless there is a good chance of resolving it through the role play. An option is to select a similar problem that exemplifies the attitudes and skills needed to solve it.

Dimensions of Role-Play Structure

We can identify at least four common dimensions of role-play structure: the extent of active involvement, the degree of situational structure, the amount of role multiplicity, and the degree of nonverbal emphasis. Each of these is discussed below.

Extent of Active Involvement

A role play can be acted out by several groups at once or by only one group. The total number of participants will affect the facilitator's decision about which design to use; it is obvious that one could not have four role-play groups of five persons each if the total number of participants were ten. However, the role-play design typically does allow the facilitator a choice regarding the extent of active involvement.

Multiple-Group Role Playing

In the *multiple role play,* several groups or pairs are established. These groups then act out the same role play simultaneously—often in the same room. These groups may or may not include observers. If they do, they usually receive reports from their observers while still in the small groups. Then these reports, or the most cogent aspects of them, are reported back to the total group in a large, general session. This type of role play is probably the most common and, in general, is easier to handle and discuss. In addition, it has certain advantages.

- If the total group is too large for all members to participate in one role play, it gives maximum opportunity for everyone to participate, to try out new attitudes and behaviors.
- It involves all members of the participant group in the problem. This helps shy or reticent group members (or those who are concerned because they have not role played before) to overcome these feelings and become involved. Because all group members are interacting, all are taking similar risks, eliminating the embarrassment of being singled out and the need to "save face."
- If observer feedback is given in the small groups, it is not as embarrassing to individual role players. If all members of

the group have a chance to participate, no individual feels singled out for evaluation and criticism.

- It enables comparisons to be made of the data from each group. Discussing each group's experiences and relating them to various actions of the role players is especially helpful. Because the roles are the same for all groups, participants realize that differences in outcome result from variations in group interactions.

Single-Group Role Playing

The *single-group role play,* however, in which one pair or group carries out the role play "on stage," in front of an audience, is especially appropriate for small groups (fewer than ten people). It also has several advantages, no matter what the size of the group.

- Because there are multiple observers, role players profit from the analytical discussion of their behaviors. People are often unaware of the effect of their actions on others and are more apt to believe several members with similar reactions than they would just one.
- Because all participants observe the same performance, it is possible to discuss the details that led to a particular effect. For example, the group can discuss the first appearance of defensive behavior on the part of one role player and then attempt to determine what behavior on someone else's part might have stimulated it.
- It aids in diagnosing the feelings of others through observation of their behavior. For example, if a person in the role play indicates that he will improve his work, the observers may be asked to comment on whether or not they believe that he means it. The role player then can be asked to report his true feelings, allowing the observers to check on the keenness of their observation skills.

- It is possible to stop the action at critical points and start again. Because only one set of behaviors occurs, the details that have been observed by everyone can be discussed, and individual role players can be given highly focused, immediate feedback on their behavior.
- It permits audience members to develop observational skills and to serve as external consultants to the role players. When a role play is stopped, some type of consultation can be used to start the role players on a different track.
- It is particularly useful for advanced or intensive training as well as for demonstrations of particular behaviors.

Single-group role playing gives the facilitator much more control over the role-play process and allows him or her to capitalize on what happens in the role play without losing sight of the learning goals.

Several variations of the single-group role play can be employed. These include:

- *Demonstrations or modeling.* Two volunteers or selected participants enact the situation while the other participants take notes and prepare to critique the interaction. The interaction then may be repeated with other role players.
- *Spontaneous role plays.* Role-play opportunities arise when someone is attempting to explain how a situation should be handled or when there is disagreement about whether a certain approach will work. The facilitator can say, "Let's experiment: you play the boss/employee/customer, and Pat will play the employee/supervisor/salesperson and will respond in the manner described."

As mentioned above, large groups can be divided into subgroups, and multiple role plays can be conducted simultaneously. This results in comparisons of processes and outcomes that provide rich data. However, it generally is *not* a good idea to have one group conduct the role play while the others merely watch. With the exception of those participants designated as observers and briefed on their function, all group members should have an opportunity to participate. Observers, especially those who have been coached on their role, are very useful in commenting on what happens during role plays.

Neither the single-group or the multiple-group role play is inherently preferable. They simply meet different training needs. The decision to use one procedure or another should be determined by the specific training objectives and the size of the group.

Degree of Situational Structure

A second dimension centers on the degree to which the role-play situation is structured. At one extreme a *scripted skit* calls for role players to act out their roles from a line-by-line script. This has the advantage of producing a highly focused demonstration, but the impact of the participants' spontaneous involvement in their roles is minimal.

Skit completion begins with a highly structured reading of lines but, at some point (often a conflict point), the script ends and the participants continue spontaneously. Perhaps the most common degree of structure is represented by the *dramatized case,* which is read silently and individually by each role player. The case may be in the form of a script, but more often simply is a page or so of background material. Role players pick up on the action in a spontaneous way, at the point at which the case leaves off. Both these approaches determine events up to a certain point, thereby controlling to some degree the type of problem or conflict that is experienced and dealt with. The higher the degree of structure, the more certain it is that specifically defined learning points will be made; however, it is possible that the participants' personal experiential involvement will be lower.

In unstructured or developmental role playing, there are no pre-prepared role instructions or background materials. The focus and structure of the role play is developed by the group as it discusses the issues and problems it wants to explore. This type of role playing calls for more sophistication and familiarity with the technology on the part of both the facilitator and the participant group, but it can be highly rewarding. Chapters 4 and 5 of this book will present more of the differences between structured and unstructured role playing and will provide guidelines for conducting both.

It is desirable in many settings to use structured role plays to obtain predictability, to aid group members in developing skill and knowledge, and to enable participants to feel comfortable in role-play situations. Within this context, an unstructured session occasionally may be interjected or—if the facilitator feels comfortable and confident working with a given group over a relatively long period of time—the sessions may gradually become increasingly unstructured as the participants become more experimental, more open, and more spontaneous in relating to interpersonal or organizational problems.

Amount of Role Multiplicity

The third dimension of role-play structure is the degree of role multiplicity. For example, it often is desirable to have one or more persons act as backups or "alter egos" to a particular role player. This often is called "doubling." A kind of minimum condition would be assigning observers to be limited alter egos for a multiple role play. At the other extreme, an audience can be divided so that each segment identifies with one of the actors in a single-group, on-stage role play. The alter ego or "double" can coach the role player to help him or her to analyze a situation more objectively, can help keep the actor "in role," can provide support for the role player in difficult situations, and can step in and change places with the role player, if desirable. Using one or more alter egos actively involves more participants in the role play and is advantageous from that viewpoint. This technique and others are discussed in more detail in Chapter 5, "Role-Play Techniques."

Degree of Nonverbal Emphasis

Finally, an often-neglected dimension concerns the degree of nonverbal emphasis in the role-play situation. Role plays can be used to focus exclusively on nonverbal behavior, through the use of pantomime for all communication, for example. Although this would generate awareness of nonverbal factors in interpersonal behavior, a more realistic approach might involve explicit role instructions that include directions about nonverbal behavior. Observers' instructions, too, can be designed to focus on this dimension.

Combinations

The four dimensions described here are independent and they can be combined in almost any imaginable way. A multiple role play could be designed with an incomplete (open-ended) script, using two alter egos and concerning scripted nonverbal behaviors. Equally possible is a single-group, on-stage design using a dramatized case with everyone but the role players being observers and with nonverbal behavior left unexamined. In addition, there are several "techniques" or ways of structuring the roles and content of the role-play design to produce certain dynamics during the role-play enactment. These techniques are discussed in Chapter 5. The specific nature of any role-play design will depend on the learning goals, the specific content issues, the nature of the population, and the facilitator's preferences, along with other factors. Awareness of these dimensions and the range of choices they imply should help the facilitator in the design process.

Dimensions of Role-Play Structure

Extent of Active Involvement

Single Group   Multiple Group

◄───►

Degree of Situational Structure

Unstructured/Developmental   Structured

◄───►

| *Straight/* | | *Dramatized* | *Skit* | | *Scripted* |
| *Demonstration* | | *Case* | *Completion* | | *Skit* |

Amount of Role Multiplicity

Individual Role   Shared Role

◄───►

Monodrama,	*Mirroring*	*Role Rotation,*	*Multiple*	*Teams*
Empty Chair,		*Role Reversal,*	*Alter Ego/*	*Play*
Soliloquy		*Single Alter*	*Group*	*Roles*
		Ego/ Doubling,	*Doubling*	
		Tag Team		

Degree of Nonverbal Emphasis

Nonverbal   Verbal

◄───►

Pantomime	*Verbal with*	*No Emphasis*
	Emphasis on	*on Nonverbal*
	Nonverbal	

Development of Role-Play Materials

It is important to develop clear, concise, and highly focused materials for use in a role play. These materials will be of two kinds: information and directions for the facilitator and information and directions for the participants.

Materials for the Facilitator

A special section of notes for the facilitator should state the purpose or possible goals of the role play, including training outcomes and behavioral objectives, that is, when the role play would be used and what the facilitator can expect to achieve by using it. The design of the role play and all accompanying materials should relate directly to and reinforce the critical problems and objectives that have been identified.

The facilitator's notes should include statements about the length of time required to conduct and process the role play (including any time needed for replaying), the degree of skill needed by the participants to engage in and process the role play, and the minimum and maximum numbers of participants. A step-by-step description should be provided for setting up the role-playing scene, and instructions should be provided for conducting the role-play itself.

If there are any unusual aspects of the role-play design (e.g., for some reason, observers are not to receive background materials prior to observing the role play), the facilitator should be informed of this in the step-by-step directions for conducting the role play. In some role-play designs, information in addition to the original background materials and role instructions is to be provided to the participants at intervals during the actual role play. Such materials, in the form of "bulletins," "telegrams," "letters," notes, etc., are used to affect the role play as it progresses. If the facilitator is to introduce such materials into the role play, he or she should be told which materials are to be used and to whom and when each is to be presented. The notes also may suggest when the facilitator might want to introduce discussions of key issues.

The notes for the facilitator also may contain suggestions for facilitating the processing discussion after the role play has been acted out. This section may contain comments about the events and results that are most likely to occur in the role play and hints about how these might be discussed. It also can present the principles involved in the case and the kinds of skills required for dealing with the problems. (See "Role Playing and the Experiential Learning Cycle" in Chapter 4, "Conducting Role Plays.")

The facilitator also should have a copy of all materials to be handed out to the participants and observers. The following is an example of typical materials for the facilitator.

SAMPLE INSTRUCTIONS FOR THE FACILITATOR[1]

"Handling Disagreement Through Effective Listening"

Goal (stated to the group)

To increase the ability of supervisors and managers to listen effectively when confronted with disagreement or resistance.

Behavioral Objectives

1. Participants will increase their skill in using questions, general statements, paraphrasing, and other nondirective or active-listening responses, specifically when confronted with feelings or ideas with which they may disagree.

2. Supervisors will increase their capacity to give and receive feedback without judgment or defensiveness.

---

[1]These instructions have been condensed to illustrate key elements. For more examples of structured role plays, see the Appendix in Shaw, Corsini, Blake, and Mouton (1980) and the cases in Maier, Solem, and Maier (1975).

Instructions (for the facilitator)

1. After a brief discussion of the purpose of the session, each participant is given either printed or verbal role-play instructions (see the sample that follows), then a brief, printed, background information sheet, if appropriate to the role play. The group then is divided into subgroups of three members each.

Sample Role-Play Instructions

During the role play, you will be asked to act out a situation, but you are not being asked to become a professional actor. It is better if you simply act as you would if you were in the position of the person described in your role instructions, as if it were "for real." For example, if you are in the role of a production manager, consider yourself to *be* the production manager rather than acting the way you *think* a production manager would. You may be asked to accept certain facts about your length of service, sex, family, affiliations, and previous experiences. Adopt these as your own and let your feelings and attitudes change as these imagined events or factors require.

During the course of the role play, issues or questions may arise that are not covered by your role instructions. If this occurs, feel free to make up facts that are appropriate to the circumstances. For example, if someone in the role play asks you how your wife or husband is, you may answer normally without altering the spirit of the role-play case. Do not make up facts that are inconsistent with your role.

---

2. One member of each subgroup is designated as member A, another as member B, and the third as the observer. Each member is given a sheet of appropriate role instructions, and the observer is provided with a pencil and lapboard or other writing surface. Questions about role instructions are answered before the role play begins.

3. Members A and B in each group conduct the role play while member C observes. (If appropriate to the design, members A and B may switch roles and replay the scene, or may receive feedback from the observer and retry it using different approaches.)

4. A discussion of the role play is conducted, drawing out observer and participant comments in order to clarify the nature of the listening process and ways in which diverse viewpoints can be pursued. Discussion items include:

  a. Which responses by Member A seemed to encourage Member B to talk more and to be more open?

  b. What comments seemed to discourage Member B or put him or her on the defensive?

  c. Were the observer and member B quickly able to discern Member A's opinions, or did he or she maintain an open listening posture?

  d. Construct a list of the kinds of comments, approaches, and attitudes that seem to improve the quality of listening.

Role Instructions for Participants

Role instructions for Members A and B and the observer are as follows:

Role Instructions for Member A

Your partner (role player B) will initiate a discussion with you. Your task during the role-playing phase of this activity is to listen and ask questions without pursuing your own opinion or attempting to force the other person into a conclusion that agrees with your own. You may, from time to time, state ideas; however, you are not to attempt to change the other person's point of view. Your goal is to listen and understand. The following information may guide you in this effort.

Appropriate Listening Responses

  1. General questions (e.g., "What do you think?" "What happened?") are useful finding out more about what another person thinks. Loaded questions or questions that lead to a predetermined answer (e.g., "Don't you think that...?") are inappropriate.

  2. Statements that encourage the person to talk (e.g., "Tell me more about it") tend to increase communication.

  3. Paraphrasing or "mirroring" the other person's statements or giving nondirective responses that pick up what the other person has said can be useful. For example, if a person says, "I think women are becoming too aggressive in trying to get ahead," you might respond, "I see, you think that women are abrasive in the way in which they are pursuing their goals." This kind of reply encourages the other person to talk and to expand or clarify the statement.

Role Instructions for Member B

During the role-play situation, you are to express your opinions freely. If you encounter resistance or disagreement, you may deal with it in any way you see fit. You are asked not to play a part but to express your genuine feelings about the issue and to pursue your point of view in order to clarify the issue, influence the other person's opinion, or simply get your own position stated. You are to initiate the discussion by introducing your point of view about this statement: *Women are treated unfairly in most organizations. Males dominate and often are unaware of their chauvinistic behavior.*

Observer Guide

During the course of the role play, observe Member A. Does he or she (check statements that apply):

_____   Quickly reveal his or her own point of view and push for it?

_____   Ask leading or loaded questions that suggest a desired answer?

_____   Seem interested in drawing out and understanding Member B's point of view?

_____   Occasionally paraphrase what Member B said or use other non-directive techniques to draw out additional information?

Comment on ways in which Member A kept the discussion going.

Materials for the Participants

Each participant, whether role player or observer, should receive an introduction to the role play, containing a *description of the general problem or situation*. In many cases, this introduction also contains a statement of the goals and issues that will be confronted during the role play. This usually is handed out to role players and observers and may be read aloud by the facilitator. This lets everyone know, at the same time, the same degree of background information. This information is separate from the individual role instructions. Ordinarily this consists of some *background data*—a scenario—to set the scene for the participants and any observers. In a business role play, for example, this data could include the name of the company, the names and positions of the role players, and any general historical or background information that is to be known to all role players and observers (whatever would be known to all members of the company in the situation to be role played). All participant materials, including background information, should be readable and not too lengthy or too complicated for a participant to remember.

Information about how the role play will be conducted and what the participants can expect to happen can be written and distributed to participants or it can be announced verbally by the facilitator. Whether written instructions are needed will depend on how complicated or detailed the role-play design is.

The *role descriptions* (a separate one for each role player) should be written in uncomplicated language and should include some hints about how to play the role. A role description may be limited to the name and description of the actual role that the participant will play, along with information about who the other participants are, or it may include attitudes, values, preferences, agenda items, and/or other characteristics to be depicted by the role player.

Most often, an individual role player will not know what information is contained in the role descriptions given to other role players. The role player should be told whether particular information pertaining to his or her character (such as hidden agendas, special information, etc.) is to be kept secret or revealed in the course of the role play. The role description also should state explicitly whether the role player is to (a) act as he or she would in real life, (b) adhere strictly to the role instructions/description, or (c) act as the role description indicates but change his/her position if appropriate as the role play progresses. The first and last choices are the ones most often preferred.

In writing the role descriptions and background information, it is important to include everything that the role players need to know in order to "get into" their roles. It also is important *not* to include much more. Role players easily can be overwhelmed by historical and numerical data and can put unnecessary energy into remembering such details. It usually is best if details are generalized as much as possible. In a business role play, company data such as a hierarchical chart and other neccessary figures can be provided in written form for the role players to refer to during the enactment. In an actual business situation, people would be likely to have such information in written form. If the role is of a "recently appointed" manager, so much the better. In this way, detailed knowledge is not required of role player.

In most role-play designs, background data sheets need to be provided for all observers—those persons in the "audience" who will not act in the role play. It also is highly desirable for observers to have *observation forms,* paper-and-pencil instruments to focus their reactions. Without such forms, there may be a tendency for observers to overpersonalize their observations and to fail to focus on the specific learnings intended. These forms may simply leave room for specific observations to be noted or they may contain tables for the collection of data, especially if results from several groups will be compared. If this is the case, sample tables should be included to illustrate how the data is to be recorded.

In unstructured/developmental role playing, a more free-form of role playing, participants create their own roles instead of using prepared, written role materials. In this case, the participants should receive an instruction sheet telling them how to proceed in defining the critical elements of the situation and in developing interactions that will explore and expand on the situation. Although this approach minimizes the need for printed materials, it often is more difficult for the facilitator to handle, in that the outcome is less predictable and may not be consistent with the expressed learning goals. This type of role playing will be discussed further in Chapters 4 and 5.

In summary, the following are things to consider when developing a role play:

Problem Situation

- Does role-play problem situation relate to group's learning needs/further group's training goals?
- Do role players have an opportunity to behave effectively?

Structure

- Extent of Active Involvement (multiple group vs. single group)
- Degree of Situational Structure (structured vs. unstructured/developmental role play)
- Amount of Role Multiplicity (individual vs. shared roles)
- Degree of Nonverbal Emphasis

Materials for Facilitator

- Notes for Facilitator (goals, training outcomes and behavioral objectives, timing, minimum and maximum group size, physical setting, preparation, step-by-step instruction for role play, facilitating and processing guidelines)
- Introduction to Role-Play (background information for participants)
- Role Instructions/Descriptions for All Role Players
- Any Background Data Sheets for Role Players and/or Observers
- Observers' Instructions/Guide
- Handouts/Lecturette Materials

Materials for Participants

- Introduction to Role Play (description of problem situation, scenario, background information)
- Role Instructions/Descriptions (a separate sheet for each role player)
- Any Background Data Sheets for Role Players and/or Observers
- Observers' Instructions/Guide
- Topical Handouts (printed lecturettes, theoretical input, models)

The Classic Role Play: Maier's "The New Truck Dilemma"

A well-known, excellent role-play design is Norman R.F. Maier's "The New Truck Dilemma," in *The Role-Play Technique* (Maier, Solem, & Maier, 1975). The learning point—conceptual, with a secondary, skill-building focus—can be stated as follows: Problem situations can be categorized in terms of (1) the requirements regarding the quality of the solution and (2) the importance of acceptance of the solution by those who must carry it out. Situations in which the latter issue is predominant typically are questions of fairness. In such cases the group leader obtains the best results by acting as a facilitator rather than as an active participant and by allowing group members to arrive at a mutually acceptable (and fair) solution. In summary, the learning objectives of this role play are:

1. To provide experiential groundwork for understanding the quality/acceptance dimensions of problem solving.
2. To demonstrate the positive effects of nondirective, facilitative leadership in a problem situation in which acceptance is the primary issue.

The stimulus materials are brief roles and a description of the situation to induce appropriate role sets. Participants become telephone servicepersons who are meeting with their boss. The roles give each person a reason for wanting a new truck that has become available; the supervisor is told to let the workers make the decision. In most groups, the desired behaviors occur as a result of the role-instruction materials. When such behaviors do not occur, the common reason is the supervisor's insistence on making the decision. In this case, however, the results also illustrate the learning point, though in a negative way.

When all groups have finished role playing, the "supervisors" report results, which are tabulated on a simple chart prepared by the facilitator during the last few minutes of the role play. These results are then discussed by the entire group, with the facilitator drawing out the learnings.

The complete text of "The New Truck Dilemma" is presented in Appendix 2 at the end of this book. Anyone who is interested in writing role plays might benefit from studying this classic case.

4

Conducting Role Plays

The Cycle of Change

Unfreezing

Most people's behavioral patterns are habitual or "frozen." Little thought is given to the approach or procedure. As a result, individuals may not realize that their behavior in a given case is inappropriate or ineffective.

In role playing, awareness of untested assumptions is heightened, and people have a chance to test the effects on others of their assumptions and behavior. As awareness grows, members of the role-playing group become self-conscious, and old behavioral patterns are "unfrozen." This examination of old patterns and the anxiety that accompanies it is a crucial step in opening up to change.

Changing

The next steps in the change cycle are: developing an understanding of the problem or ineffective behavior; developing several alternative actions or behaviors that might resolve the problem; and actually trying out one or more of these alternatives. Role playing is an excellent means of accomplishing these steps. Once the individual understands the need for change, he or she must explore the situation in order to develop alternative solutions that have a reasonable chance of being successful. Acting out the problem situation is an excellent way to examine and explore it.

In a role play, people can *try* out new behaviors in a safe setting and determine which alternatives work best. They can receive constructive feedback from others and can *practice* behaviors and try variations. Thus, long periods of real-life time can be simulated in a few role-playing sessions.

Refreezing

When people practice new behavior in a role-play setting, they are more apt to try it later in real-life situations. Employing the new behavior in actual life situations is the only way to accomplish the third part of the change process, refreezing. When the parties involved in the role-play are the same ones as those in the real-life situation, there is even greater likelihood that the changed behavioral pattern will be successful and will continue over time, because all parties have changed expectations and because they *support* the change effort. Support or reinforcement for new behavior is very important in sustaining it.

As participants become used to engaging in role plays, they will take less time to unfreeze. As they become comfortable with the technique, they will become more flexible and experimental, better able to test assumptions and to explore and experiment with new procedures and behaviors. They also will learn to give constructive, accurate, feedback to others and will provide more effective support for change.

Preparing for Role Playing

In order to realize the maximum learning potential of the role-play technique, the facilitator should be aware of some special considerations in utilizing this technology. Perhaps the most important is to keep the objectives of the role play and the facilitator's role clear throughout the entire process. The facilitator needs to be confident that the objectives are being met and that the activities can be focused adequately within a narrow range of learning goals. Toward this end, it is helpful if the participants as well as the organization are involved in setting goals for the session.

Participant involvement in planning the role-play session helps to create a sense of ownership in the outcomes and also helps to clarify the methodology. Participants often can suggest key problem situations, issues, and areas for practice and guidance. This information can be gathered before the training session by means of interviews, questionnaires, or small-group discussions.

From the beginning, it is important for the facilitator to prepare for the role play by establishing the proper mood and expectations, keeping the objectives continuously clear, and making certain that the entire experience has an obvious logic to it. The importance of establishing a proper mind set early cannot be overemphasized. Because the term "role playing" can connote "fun and games" for some people, it is up to the facilitator to establish that the activity is intended to promote learning. The nature of the role play and the objectives should be specified beforehand, except in a situation intended to explore covert interpersonal processes, such as the use and impact of hidden agendas. Even in such a case, however, the facilitator needs to keep the training objectives in mind at all times.

Size of Groups

The size of the group usually will range from ten to fifty participants. The ideal size for single-group role playing is around twelve to fifteen; for multiple-group role playing it is between twenty-five and fifty. The skill and experience of the facilitator and the size of the room also must be taken into consideration. If these are optimal, a larger group can be handled for each type of role playing.

Managing Differences in Rank

It generally is not a good idea to mix people of different rank who work together. Differences in status create attitudes and affect that can be brought into the training situation and can affect the interaction. This may not be true in a relatively small organization in which all personnel are well acquainted with one another and respond to one another's personalities rather than to their positions. The problem of rank also is affected by the attitudes of the people involved. If the training group is composed of people from different organizations who do not know one another, or if the facilitator is sure enough of his or her skills and of the nonthreatening nature of the role play to be used, differences in rank may not matter. If the facilitator thinks that they would matter, it would be wise to choose a training technology other than role playing.

On the other hand, it usually is a good idea to have a mixture of people from similar-level jobs but from different departments or divisions within an organization. This helps the participants to learn that other people have situations and problems similar to their own. It allows the exchange of opinions and experiences that can enrich the training. It also contributes to a better understanding of the other parts of the organization and a networking function across levels. These effects can improve communication, help in the development of a broader view of the organization, and ease the process of lateral transfers.

Accommodating Both Sexes

The presence of both men and women in a role play is probably more of a benefit than a problem. A person can take the role of a member of the opposite sex if necessary, but more often the role description merely can be changed to fit the sex of the role player. If the role play is to focus on sexual issues or stereotypes, it can be conducted first with all participants playing members of their *own* sex and then repeated with men and women exchanging roles and playing members of the *opposite* sex.

Physical Accommodations

The room need only be large enough to comfortably accommodate the action and the observers, if there are any. Even when multiple role playing is going on, the noise from adjacent groups tends to stimulate the action rather than detract from it. In general, "large enough" means twenty-five to fifty square feet per participant. A room that is only slightly too small is preferable to one that is clearly too large.

The room should be located to minimize distractions such as telephones and voices. Care should be taken so that "outsiders"—people who are not participating in the role play—do not enter the room, look in, or overhear the role play.

The most important criterion for furniture is flexibility. Many role plays call for basic "props" such as a table and chairs to represent desks, conference tables, desk chairs, sofas, etc. The physical props need not be elaborate; the role players can use their imaginations.

Movable chairs also allow participants to form groups of varying size for role playing, observation, and discussion. This permits maximum visual and verbal communication among members of the group. If a room with movable chairs is not available, another option is to use an actual office in which the furniture lends itself to the requirements of the role play. If the group is large, auditorium seating is all right if there is a stage area with movable furniture available for role playing. This at least will ensure that all observers can see all aspects of the role play.

The facilitator will want to have newsprint flip charts and easels on which to place them, felt-tip markers, and masking tape for posting sheets of newsprint containing lists, posters, etc. that result from the group's discussions.

Each observer should be furnished with a portable writing surface such as a lapboard or notebook on which to take notes and with paper (or observation forms) and pens or pencils.

Introducing the Role Play

Climate Setting

The first step in beginning the training session is introducing oneself appropriately, telling the participants that they will be participating in a role play and why, and briefly describing what will happen during the event.

The next, critical, step is establishing an open, experimental climate. If participants do not have experience in role playing, they may feel uncomfortable about "making fools of themselves in front of other people." It is important to allow them to become acquainted with one another and to establish a climate of support and experimentation before initiating a role play. If the participants do not know one another, getting-acquainted activities may be conducted to "warm up" the group.

It is extremely important that the feedback to be given to role players by other role players and observers be constructive and useful. Guidelines for giving and receiving feedback (Hanson, 1975, 1981) can be distributed and discussed before the role play, as part of the introduction of norms and standards for the training session. For your convenience, these guidelines are reprinted in Appendix 3 at the end of this book.

People are likely to be unwilling to participate in a role play if past experience has shown them that the role play is used as a basis for free-for-all criticism and evaluation. When people feel incompetent, defensive, or angry, they are not apt to be open to learning. The preparation for the role play should include a statement by the facilitator about the purpose of feedback and the ways in which it is to be used during the session.

Group members also must understand the topics, problems, and principles with which they will be dealing and the norms and standards under which they will be operating. In most cases, the goals or objectives of the session should be specified. The participants then can be asked to identify their own personal objectives for the session, whether they be the acquisition of knowledge or skill or the development of more effective attitudes and feelings. Participants should be encouraged to "buy into" the role-play experience. The group members' feelings as well as their thoughts must be involved if the role play is to be realistic and effective.

If appropriate, a lecturette, videotape, or other technique can be used to define key issues and focus the group's attention on problems that will be addressed during the role play. For example, a film on performance review, meeting management, or sales techniques could be presented, and the group members then could be asked to discuss the principles presented and to examine the quality of interaction portrayed on the screen. The facilitator can ask questions such as "How do you feel when. . . ?," "What has happened in your past experience with this topic that made it easy for you to respond/participate. . .,?" and "What do you think are the most important considerations/things to do when you are engaged in a discussion of. . . ?" Key points can be listed on a newsprint poster. This type of discussion can help group members to become more aware of the principles, techniques, and problems encountered in the topic of the role play. Such awareness can help to increase their readiness to re-examine past experiences and practice new skills. In some cases, the discussion can serve as the basis for the role-play format, and the observers' guidelines can include tallies and descriptions of the key behaviors that have been identified by the group.

In structured role playing, the format for the role play is preplanned and assigned by the facilitator. For example, the facilitator may outline a procedure for handling customer complaints, such as (a) listen to the customer, (b) get details about the complaint, (c) indicate policy while remaining polite and helpful, (d) suggest a course of action. Some group members then would be asked to play the role of the complaining customer while others play the organizational representative.

Assigning Roles

In setting up the situation, it is important to give an overview to establish who is going to be involved and how. Participants can be selected by one of four basic models: using volunteers, typecasting participants on the basis of their personalities, making assignments on the basis of some other knowledge of participants, and utilizing role reversals. The latter might, for example, involve having someone with high status play a low-status position and vice versa. Roles (including that of observer) can be assigned by having group members count off, then announcing "Member number one in each group will play the employee, member two will play the supervisor, member three will serve as observer," etc.

If multiple-group role playing is to be employed, small groups are formed, as appropriate to the number of participants present and the number needed for each role-play group. Roles are assigned within each group. The participants are informed that each group will enact the same role play and that all groups will conduct the enactment simultaneously. Additional facilitators may be needed if there are several groups.

After participants understand whether they are to be role players or observers, and how they will be grouped, the facilitator can hand out the written background sheets and role instructions and allow adequate time for the participants to read them. The facilitator should be thoroughly familiar with all role-play materials before attempting to use them with a group. The facilitator then can answer questions and consult with any participants who have special role instructions. The facilitator should make it clear that the role players will not be allowed to re-examine their roles once the interaction has begun. In briefing role players, the facilitator should not make the mistake of assuming that people know how to get into their roles; a bit of coaching on role taking may be necessary.

A very effective way of briefing role players is to designate support individuals or groups that can function as coaches during caucusing sessions. These groups can be established either randomly or through volunteering, and they can provide each role player with a support base for getting into and staying in role. A variation on the support group is the reference group, consisting of participants with similar jobs. For example, secretaries in a workshop could be the reference group for an individual who is going to role play a secretary.

In instructing participants on how to role play, Maier, Solem, and Maier's (1975) seven directions, as outlined below, are useful.

1. Accept and adopt the facts of the role.
2. *Be* the role.
3. You may change your attitude(s) during the action.
4. Let yourself become emotionally aroused.
5. Make up data, if necessary, but do not alter the spirit of the case.
6. Avoid consulting your role notes during the role play.
7. Do not overact; it may detract from the learning goals.

These instructions also can be reproduced on the role-description sheets that are handed out to role players prior to the activity. The role instructions should clarify whether role players are to (a) act as they personally would in such a situation, (b) act as their character is described in the role instructions, or (c) remain true to the character as generally described but take it from there as the situation develops.

Before actually beginning the role play, the facilitator should allow time for the participants to think privately in order to assume the characters of their roles. It also is a good idea describe the procedure and read all instructions before people begin to role play. If they are interrupted after they are "into the swing of things," they may not be able to re-establish their mood.

Briefing Observers

In briefing observers, it is important to clarify their tasks. Are they simply observers or are they permitted to talk with one another?

Are they expected to make a report after the role play? Are they going to meet with individuals? It is preferable to provide observers with printed observation sheets, generally in instrument format. Any such forms for recording observations should be explained. If the observers are to be permitted to intervene in the role play with process observations, this procedure should be made explicit. If the observers are to function as alter egos, this role probably should be demonstrated by the facilitator. In the example given previously of a customer complaint scenario, half the observers in a group might be asked to observe the complaining customer's behavior and report on what they perceive to be his or her feelings, attitudes, and concerns, while the other half of the observers watch the member who is handling the complaint and report on that person's feelings, attitudes, concerns, and behaviors.

Directing the Action

Staging

Once the role players and observers are familiar with their roles, the actual interchange can begin. In staging a role play, several arrangements suggest themselves. The "group-on-group" role play, conducted in the center of the room with observers circled around it, increases the sense of involvement Alternatively, the role play can be staged with the observers in a semicircular arrangement so that the role players can be seen from the front. In multiple-group role plays, each group should be arranged in such a way that it can interact with minimal interruption from the other groups. If there are several groups, or if the role play is likely to be fairly noisy, the role plays can be conducted in separate rooms.

Timing

Most role plays are conducted for specific periods of time. In some designs, the actors play their roles until resolution is achieved or time is called. In other designs, the action is either stopped after a specified amount of time or completed, then the players *exchange* roles, and the role players begin again from the start. This provides an opportunity to explore the situation from another person's point of view. Other variations call for the action to be stopped so the role players can describe their thoughts and feelings and so the observers or role players can comment on how the role play is going and make suggestions about what the role players might do or might have done to improve the communication or situation. Then the role play begins again with the participants in the same roles but trying new skills/strategies, alternative ways for dealing with the situation. In any case, the facilitator should give adequate time warnings.

Facilitating

A structured role play is directed by the design itself, by the role instructions, background information, and so on that are provided. The facilitator rarely intervenes except for procedural matters or interventions that are part of the role-play structure. (See the discussion that follows on the use of such interventions.) However, the facilitator must be aware of what is likely to happen in the role play and must have a sense of the relative importance of situations and events. He or she must use tact and sensitivity in dealing with the role players as they work through problem situations. The ability to simplify or straighten out complexities, persuasiveness, and the ability to help people to see and understand what is going on are key facilitator attributes. The facilitator must keep participants interested and involved as well as help them to assess the situation and make good decisions. By *modeling openness, sincerity, and concern for the feelings of others,* the facilitator will help the participants to function together effectively.

While the role play is being conducted, the facilitator must be able to modulate the intensity of the event. This can be effected in a number of ways. Humor can be used to lighten a heavy interaction; the role play can be put "on hold"; participants can be assigned different roles during the role play; the interaction can be stimulated through intervention on the part of the facilitator; or role players can be instructed to remain in their roles. The facilitator can tell participants to reread their role descriptions and coach one another on roles, and then there can be interim caucuses between observers and support or reference groups and/or the role players. What the facilitator should *not* do is act as "expert" and tell the participants what to do. Role playing is effective for participants because it is highly experiential. For this reason also, the role play should be ended before it either becomes boring or loses its focus on the learning goals.

In some role-play designs, an element of deception may be built in in order to heighten learnings about listening, leadership, cooperation, information sharing, etc. In such situations, some participants may be unaware of the roles, hidden agendas, or information assigned to other role players. The facilitator must be prepared to process this type of "manipulation" and must weigh the use of such activities in terms of benefits versus backlash.

It is important for the facilitator to be thorough in working all the way through the experiential learning cycle explained later in this chapter. Forms and guided procedures can be extremely helpful for publishing experiential data, but the facilitator must assist the participants in using the forms and by explaining and tracking the procedures.

Using Interventions

Interventions are built into many structured role plays. These interventions have numerous purposes: they may be designed to add interest to the role play, to stimulate or challenge the role players, to allow participants to experience different points of view, or to allow for the sharing of feedback and information. Typical interventions are as follows.

1. *Observers.* One or more people are assigned various observation functions during the role play. In multiple-group role playing, it is typical to have two people enact a role-play dialog (e.g., manager-subordinate, salesperson-customer, etc.) while other members of the group observe the interaction, taking notes as they watch. Observers usually have prepared formats for note taking and reporting; these guidelines reflect the issues and goals of the session. In some designs, each observer is instructed to observe a specific role player; in others, each observer is instructed to observe

a specific type of behavior. The possibilities for using observers are great, and should be suited to the objectives of the session and the nature of the role play itself.

2. *Role Rotation.* In order to expose various dimensions of the problem and to contrast various techniques, approaches, and styles, role players may be asked to rotate or exchange roles. In a demonstration role play, the key player (the one with the presenting problem or message) may be asked to take on the role of the responding player to demonstrate his or her understanding of that role as it was portrayed in the previous enactment. In multiple role playing, it often is useful to have members of each role-playing group rotate positions (for example, the manager becomes the subordinate, the subordinate becomes the observer, and the observer becomes the manager). There is some flexibility in how the exchanging or switching of roles can be accomplished; as with other interventions, it should be designed to further the understanding of the role players and the goals of the role-play session.

3. *Feedback from Role Players Themselves.* Participants in the role play may be asked to fill out reaction sheets after the role play has ended. For example, the person who played the role of a counselor can be given a response sheet designed to identify major areas of resistance and the degree to which he or she felt that empathy was established. Simultaneously, the person who played the role of counselee could be asked to answer questions from that point of view. By exchanging feedback after the enactment, the participants can become more aware of differences in perception, gaps in understanding, and opportunities for using new skills in interpersonal situations.

4. *Information Sharing.* After the role-play has ended, participants can be provided with descriptions of situations that are comparable to the one with which they have been dealing. For example, in a multiple role-play situation in which triads have been playing the roles of shop foreman, shop steward, and employee, the role players can be asked to develop a course of action based on their role-played discussion. Comparative courses of action or solutions then can

be distributed to members of the triads so that they can compare their results with the results of other groups, with "ideal" solutions, or with solutions that are compatible with union contracts. It is important to note that when "ideal" or comparative solutions are distributed, role players who have invested energy and thought into developing solutions to which they are committed may become defensive. This can be avoided by introducing contrasting (or what may look like "recommended") solutions early in the process so that group members have a chance to integrate these solutions into their own plans and to try out new approaches rather than simply to receive information after the fact.

Second Enactments

It often is desirable to provide opportunities for role-play participants to try out new techniques and new approaches, based on their experiences during the first enactment and on the feedback they have received from one another and from observers. In some cases, the second enactment is designed to allow players to switch or rotate roles. In other situations, new input is provided by means of lecturettes, videotapes, or other sources of information. During the second role play, then, participants can utilize the additional information that they have received.

In many designs, the participants begin to work on problems, stop and receive feedback, and then restart the role play. Each new attempt provides an opportunity to apply new insights, new techniques or approaches, and new information.

Deroling

It is important to remember that the initial attitudes adopted by role players may change, and change can produce several different emotions. Events in the process of role playing may alter attitudes and create pleasant or unpleasant feelings. As a result, the people involved may have some of the same emotional experiences that occur in real-life situations. This is one of the most important values in role playing and serves as a rehearsal for pratical problems. As participants become experienced in role-playing situations, they learn to feel the part, and role-playing behavior becomes more and more authentic.

The facilitator needs to help the participants to unwind after the role play has ended. A role play may become very intense or participants may identify aspects of themselves that they wish to explore further, so ample time must be allowed for them to talk together or to seek personal time with the staff members. Getting participants out of the content of the roles is crucial for effective processing.

While de-roling the role players after the role play, the facilitator may invite them to "ventilate' or to explore in an expressive way the feelings that they experienced during the activity. They also can be invited to finish unfinished business by making statements such as "If I had been the boss. . . ." Role players often can separate themselves from the role through a written analysis of the role-play situation afterwards. Sometimes this process can be stimulated by having individual consultants work with role players in order to "finish" the experience.

Feedback

In structured role-play designs, which have predetermined goals and outcomes, giving and receiving feedback generally is designed into the overall process. The instructions for the facilitator often specify where, when, and how feedback will occur.

Managing the Feedback Process

Participants need to be reminded that sometimes people do learn from experience. A golfer who slices the ball receives negative feedback on his stroke because the ball does not go where he wanted it to go. Likewise, some role-play feedback comes from the situation itself. Role players may be well aware of the fact that they have not solved a problem or that one of them has found resistance or hostility in another role player. Much learning can occur as the result of an individual's experiences during and reactions to the role play, without the added advantage of feedback from other sources.

Although feedback from others often can help to organize, relate, validate, and further refine it, personal, intuitive learning should be encouraged and drawn out for discussion. Starting the post-role-play discussion with personal reactions parallels the "publishing" phase of the experiential learning cycle and helps to warm up the participants for the process of giving and receiving feedback from one another.

On the other hand, some individuals may not be aware of the nature of their impact; they may be so wrapped up in their own actions that they fail to notice how these actions affect or appear to others. Furthermore, many skills are enhanced primarily through obtaining instruction and feedback while practicing and applying what has been learned.

Usually feedback is provided by the role players (to one another) and the observers. Role players often can give one another inter-personal feedback in role as a means of ending the activity and getting themselves beyond it in order to explore its generalizable learning. This helps them to derole and prepares them to receive feedback from the observers. Observers may have been assigned to specific role players ("observer A will watch and take notes on the performance of role player A") or they may have been instructed to watch for specific behaviors or outcomes. In some designs, the observers' reports are generalized. Feedback also can be solicited by polling the group; e.g., the facilitator can ask, "How many of you in the group would be willing to change your mind regarding the problem issue, based on the discussion that has just occurred?"

The impact of feedback can be either positive or negative. Positive feedback is supportive and affirming. Although negative feedback does have a purpose, i.e., it is information to be dealt with and usually is intended to aid in correction, it can leave an individual feeling ineffective or diminished. It is important that the facilitator create an atmosphere in which feedback can be used by explaining that feedback and other forms of post-enactment analysis are aimed at providing new insights, new opportunities, and support, rather than evaluation. *The best precaution against overly critical or unconstructive feedback is to design the feedback process so that it creates awareness and sensitivity rather than serving as a vehicle for criticism and evaluation.* Appendix 3 at the end of this book contains guidelines for giving and receiving feedback.

These can be used to prepare the participants for this important interaction.

A basic approach in managing feedback is to ask for affirmative feedback, e.g., "What are some of the things the manager did that were particularly effective?" or "In what ways did the counselor indicate his or her concern regarding the other person's feelings?" To encourage participants, both role players and observers, to focus their learning, the facilitator can instruct them to concentrate on comparing feelings with observable behavior and to develop generalizations about the worlds that they ordinarily work in, while avoiding any discussion about personalities within the role-play situation. Another approach is to focus on the procedure rather than the role player. The facilitator might say, "We spoke earlier of a four-step procedure in handling customer complaints. Which of the steps did you see demonstrated during the last role play?" Or, "Which steps do you think might have been used to greater advantage during the role play?" The facilitator also should reiterate the objectives of the activity. Often it is useful if the objectives are posted on newsprint in the training room.

The problem or situation around which the role play was designed can be examined from a theoretical point of view, the instance under examination serving as an example for further generalization. This type of discussion tends to be productive because the language is precise and can be related to actual behavior and shared experience. The facilitator needs to be particularly careful to encourage the generalizing and applying aspects of the experiential learning cycle, as these often are omitted, leaving practical, transferable learning to chance.

Types of Feedback

Feedback Against Standards or Criteria

It is not always possible to obtain feedback based on results. For example, instructors have difficulty in judging their own effectiveness because the competencies, motivations, and backgrounds of their students vary so greatly. It frequently may be necessary to establish criteria other than, or in addition to, bottom-line results.

It also is often true that inability to obtain bottom-line results may be because of performance problems or other factors that need to be identified clearly and then improved before they can contribute to basic objectives. For example, performance regarding patient care in one section of a hospital may be lower than in another section. It may be measured by patient reactions, mistakes made in dispensing medication, and other specific criteria. However, the hospital personnel in the first section may not know how to improve the quality of patient care even though they are aware that it needs to be done. It may be necessary to isolate a variety of measurable performance criteria in order to achieve a broader objective in examining patient care. The nurses may need feedback on practices in dispensing medication; aides may need training in interpersonal skills and other dimensions of their relationships with patients. In another example, to tell a salesperson "You are not making enough sales" may be inadequate feedback to aid that person in improving his or her performance. It may be necessary to identify specific performance factors such as sales prospecting, the ability to handle objections, the ability to close the sale, and so on. In applying this approach to role playing, the facilitator must establish—or engage the group in establishing—performance criteria for the procedure or skill being practiced.

Impressionistic Feedback

In many situations it is almost impossible to develop "hard" criteria for measuring performance and providing feedback. For example, a fund raiser may follow all the prescribed rules in dealing with potential donors but still admit that something is lacking. A casual observer might say, "I get the impression that you really don't enjoy your job," or "It seems to me that you just aren't enthusiastic," or "I don't think that you are a very good listener." In many cases it is possible to convert these impressions into more tangible and specific performance criteria. However, in many other situations, impressions, perceptions, and reactions are just as important as hard data. If, for example, a subordinate gives a manager the impression that the subordinate is hostile or resentful, it really does not matter very much whether it is a hard fact. The subordinate may think of himself as "shy" or "self-possessed," but if his manager sees him as "aloof" or "hostile," it is likely to cause problems for him on the job.

Role playing provides many opportunities for giving and receiving impressionistic feedback. Because many impressions can stand in the way of effective interpersonal relations or other types of effectiveness and success, the information received from this type of feedback can be very valuable.

Data-Based Feedback

There are numerous ways by which to make feedback more accurate. All involve some structured methods for recording what the role players do. These methods can range from merely having the observers write down what they see, to giving the observers written observation guides, to administering a written questionnaire to all participants during or after the role play.

The most complete record can be created by recording the role play on audio- or videotape (closed-circuit television). Although effective use of tape media requires skill and practice on the part of the facilitator, it is a powerful way to provide feedback. It is difficult for role players to deny or distort their behaviors when those behaviors are displayed audibly or visually. With videotape, both verbal and nonverbal behaviors can be reviewed. Furthermore, comparisons can be made among several role players or role-playing groups, allowing the participants to see their own behaviors in the context of a range of behaviors.

However, because these media are over-rich in information, the facilitator must be skilled in using them as feedback tools. The facilitator must know how to operate the recording and playback equipment. The participants must be prepared for the taping so that they do not act differently because their behavior is being recorded. It is a good idea to assure the group members that the tape will be erased following the feedback session. The timing also must be planned; it typically takes one or one and one-half hours to review thirty minutes of videotape. Thus, it is necessary that the facilitator carefully select the material to be reviewed. This means allotting time before the feedback session to select specific "bits" of behavior. These must be selected carefully so that they further the learning goals without appearing to present people's behavior unfavorably out of context. Even so, participants' responses to seeing or hearing themselves on tape may range from surprised to disturbed; it is important that these initial reactions are worked through so that more significant levels of learning can be explored. Finally, the facilitator must have the skill to lead the role players and the rest of the group to valid insights. It is important to avoid ridicule and nitpicking and to create a supportive and positive climate. The facilitator will need to judge the appropriate depth of feedback.

Feedback from Performance or Results

In role playing, as in many other endeavors, feedback can come from actual performance or results. This is particularly true in the case of feedback to the facilitator. If a facilitator conducts a training session, and the participants report high levels of satisfaction and seem to perform better as a result of the training, the facilitator has received positive feedback from the situation itself and from the results achieved. A facilitator who does not achieve positive results in a training session also is receiving feedback. In this case, he or she needs to re-examine his or her performance as well as the training design in order to determine what steps must be taken in order to achieve positive results. It may be necessary for the facilitator to solicit more systematic feedback or to observe other facilitators in similar sessions so that his or her performance can be improved.

Likewise, if participants in a role-play session do not achieve the results that they expect in their back-home situations, it is likely that they are not doing what they think in terms of applying the lessons from the role play. In this case, it would be wise for the participants to contact the facilitator or other participants to check assumptions and re-evaluate their "modified" behavior. It is a good idea to build into the role-play training design an opportunity for participants to report back on their progress and to ask for clarification and further help.

Analysis and Closure

In both structured and unstructured role-play sessions, closure is necessary. Participants have been through a series of experiences that suggest the possibility of changes in behavior, applications of new learnings and new skills, and the development of new ways of relating to others. It is the facilitator's job to do all that can be done within the training setting to make it possible for the participants to act on these newly surfaced concerns and objectives. Post-enactment analysis is concerned for the most part with providing feedback to individuals and giving them some indication of new directions that might be possible in handling future problems. It often is possible to organize this feedback and discussion experience into a more generalized form so that participants feel that they have a basis for future action. The discussion that follows, "Role Playing in the Experiential Learning Cycle," tells how to structure the role-play session so that participants have an opportunity to organize, codify, and apply their experiences and learnings.

Role Playing in the Experiential Learning Cycle

The actual role-playing activity is the beginning of a five-step experiential model that is based on a cyclical learning process of five separate but interlocking procedures. (A complete description of the model is found in *Using Structured Experiences in Human Resource Development,* the first book in this University Associates Training Technologies set.) As implied by the name of the model, the emphasis is on the *direct* experiences of the participant or learner, as opposed to the *vicarious* experiences garnered through didactic approaches.

The experiential model also is an inductive, rather than a deductive process: the participants *discover* for themselves the learnings offered by the experiential process. This discovery may be facilitated by a leader, but in the end the participants find and validate their own experiences.

This is the "laboratory" approach to learning. It is based on the premise that experience precedes learning and that the learning, or meaning, to be derived from any experience comes from the learner. Any individual's experience is unique to that individual; no one can tell the person what he or she is to learn or gain from any activity. Probable learnings can, of course, be devised, but it is up to the participants to validate these for themselves.

Each step of the experiential learning cycle can be related to role playing. Five revolving steps are included in the experiential model:

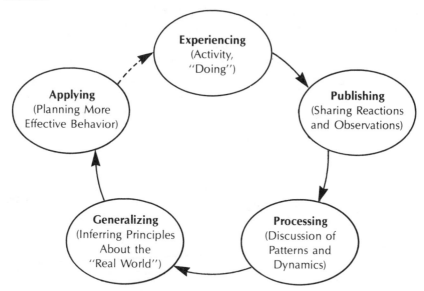

Experiencing

The process usually starts with experiencing. The participant becomes involved in an activity; he or she acts or behaves in some way or does, performs, observes, sees, or says something. This initial experience is the basis for the entire process.

In role playing, during the *experiencing* phase the focus is on the role play itself. It is important to recognize that this phase creates the data base of human interaction for later discussion. Thus, much of the emphasis in preparing a role play has to be on later phases, i.e., what happens after the role play itself is completed.

Publishing

Following the experience itself, it becomes important for each participant to share or "publish" his or her reactions and observations with others who have either experienced or observed the same activity.

In the *publishing* phase, the role players' expressions of feelings, attitudes, and experiences and the observers' reports are the significant aspects. Here the emphasis is on sharing reactions experienced in the role play. In the typical design, the person who received the problem or message gives his or her impression of how it felt and how it went. The observers are asked to comment on their reactions to that person's role. Then the person who presented the problem or message shares his or her reactions and impressions, and the observers comment on their reactions to his or her role. All group members may discuss the overall tone of the action. If there are more than two role players, the reactions of the role holders are shared first, then those of the observers.

During this phase, it is important that the participants not skip to making suggestions or drawing conclusions or principles, but stick to "feeling" reactions to the experience. The facilitator can summarize these reactions to make certain that they have been understood and then move the group into the next step.

Processing

Sharing one's reactions is only the first step. An essential—and often neglected—part of the cycle is the necessary integration of this sharing. The dynamics that emerged in the activity are explored, discussed, and evaluated (processed) with other participants.

Observers of a role play can report the patterns of behavior that they observed and make *suggestions* during this step. The facilitator can ask questions as well; for example, the person who presented the problem or message can be asked "Do you think that role player B understood your point of view?," then "Do you think that she will do anything about it?" A typical processing question is "How could communication have been enhanced or objectives achieved better?" In guiding this discussion, the facilitator will need to take into consideration the sophistication of the participants and their previous experiences in role playing.

At this point, role players often are still in their roles emotionally, and it is important to make an intervention that will help to "derole" them and make them more receptive to cognitive integration of the experience. Often a simple announcement—"All role players may now resume being and acting themselves"—is adequate. Sometimes, however, a meeting may be required with support or reference groups for the purpose of finishing the unfinished business of the role play. The use of videotaped replay in the processing phase can be highly advantageous for focusing the study of the dynamics of the role-play situation—the patterns of behavior that spontaneously emerge in the interaction of the role players.

Generalizing

Flowing logically from the processing step is the need to develop principles or extract generalizations from the experience. Stating implications and discussing learnings and new skills in this way can help participants to further define, clarify, and elaborate them. For example, during the role play and the subsequent discussion, it may have become clear that too much conversation from an interviewer tends to block effectiveness. The resulting generalization may be "It usually is inappropriate for the interviewer (or person receiving information) to dominate the conversation." Now the group can begin to develop specific principles that support the generalization. The group may even develop suggestions for action, such as the following:

- Rather than repeating your own opinion, ask questions to clarify the opinions of others.
- After you have asked a question, remain silent for ten or fifteen seconds rather than reframing your question or trying to push the other person to talk.
- Summarize the other person's point of view frequently to show that you are listening and to aid the other person in expressing or clarifying his or her ideas.

In some cases, the generalizations that have emerged can be converted into procedural form. An example of this might be a list of steps to be followed (progressive discipline) in dealing with problem employees. The principles involved in the role-play issue have been experienced in such a way that it has become possible for the facilitator or the group members to be much more specific about the meaning of the principle and the action steps that are suggested.

There are a variety of techniques for helping participants to generalize from the role-play experience to "real-world" situations. Individuals and/or groups can be instructed to write declarative statements based on their experiences outside the training situation, and participants can be encouraged to develop cause-and-effect hypotheses about the dynamics that emerged in the role-play.

Applying

The final step in the cycle is to plan applications of the principles derived from the experience. The experiential process is not complete until a new learning or discovery is used and tested behaviorally. This is the "experimental" part of the experiential model. Applying, of course, becomes an experience in itself, and, with new experience, the cycle begins again.

This final phase of the role-play process is the most important one. In this part of the design, participants are led to explore two crucial questions: "So what?" and "Now what?" These discussions can take place between goal-setting partners, within natural subgroups of the training group, between participant-observer pairs, and by repeating the role play and applying the generalizations that came out of the first round. It is important that the facilitator, in devising a role play, think very carefully about how participants are to be led from playing a role to integrating their learning into practical, everyday, significant changes in behavior.

In some instances, such as when a series of training sessions are being conducted and "follow-up" is scheduled later, the applying stage may be relatively open ended. Participants may not yet have experienced situations that are supportive of the theories of the methodology. If the role-play experience has been highly individualized or emotional, people may need to think about their experiences in the role-playing session before deciding how they will act differently in their back-home situations. At this point, there may be no basis for prescribing behavior; if the individual is acutely aware of a need to follow a given procedure or behave in a new way, the intensity of commitment may be quite clear and to impose prescriptions may well be presumptuous or may preclude further learning or insight. Even in such situations, an action commitment can be made: people can agree that they will think about the issues or read more about them or discuss them with friends or colleagues. Contracts can be made for follow-up reports at a *specified* time in the future.

Unstructured/Developmental Role Playing

The Warm-Up Phase

As described by Shaw, Corsini, Blake, and Mouton (1980), in preparing for an unstructured role play, the emphasis of the process is on the group itself. The facilitator describes the objectives of the overall session (but not of the role play) and introduces the concept of role playing and the norms of the training group. The facilitator may suggest a general, overall topic for the session, such as "handling employee complaints" or "improving interdepartmental communication." During the warm-up part of the session, the topic is discussed, and a verbal survey of pertinent problems and examples usually is conducted. Examples of survey questions are: "What are some of the major issues you have confronted in dealing with employee complaints?" and "What are some of the major obstacles you have encountered in dealing with department B?" As the discussion progresses, the facilitator checks to determine whether an *identified issue is considered to be important or significant by the majority of group members.* The discussion continues until the facilitator and group members agree that one or more key issues have been isolated and that they are worth working on. These become the issues to be addressed and/or problems to be confronted by the role play.

Just as in structured role playing, the warm-up and orientation phase of the session can include the use of films, videotapes, printed materials, simulations, and so on, to stimulate group interest, understanding, and concern about a certain issue or problem. The distinguishing thing about an unstructured role play is that the facilitator does not predetermine the relationships or processes that will take place when the role-play enactment begins. Written role descriptions, background sheets, and predetermined problems are *not* used. In unstructured role plays, participants often deal with their own concerns and relationships while working on the issues of general concern.

Facilitating

The facilitator is the major source of interventions in a developmental role play. He or she may intervene by guiding the way in which issues or situations are structured, by encouraging group discussion or feedback, or by employing any of the wide range of techniques that are described in the next chapter. Developmental role plays are highly dependent on the creativity and skill of the facilitator and on the way in which the process is managed. The facilitator must help the group members to identify problems; to move in and out of problem areas in ways that are useful and constructive; to create role flexibility, spontaneity, and creative interaction; and to use the role play to generate deeper understanding and to improve self-awareness and interpersonal skill. The facilitator uses the process and the techniques that he or she has learned to involve the participants and to encourage them to move toward experimentation with new behavior and the development of new awareness. The following are some of the interventions that can be used in developmental role playing.

Develop Consensus

The facilitator may prescribe a general theme or objective for the session but, in a developmental or unstructured process, cannot prescribe the content of the interactions. Nor can the specific situation to be dealt with be imposed on the group. Therefore, it is critical that the facilitator direct the group members to spend whatever amount of time is needed in exploring one another's concerns and problems and in identifying a group focus. The facilitator's task is to help the group to draw out a problem issue that is shared by all members. Common links must be established so that all members feel some degree of ownership of the problem.

Ask for Volunteers

One of the most common concerns of the facilitator of unstructured role plays is the problem of obtaining responsive participants.

There are numerous ways in which people can be encouraged to join the enactment comfortably and spontaneously. The first of these is asking for volunteers.

Often there are group members who are eager to try out new behaviors. Others may want to test their current methods of handling difficult situations. Still others may enjoy the opportunity to do a little "acting." The facilitator can encourage these motivations by saying something such as the following: "We have talked about some of the problems in. . . . It would be useful to all of us if someone in the group would show us some of the ways in which he or she deals with. . . ." Or "First let us define. . ., and that will move us closer to selecting a problem situation." Group members often will begin to describe issues relevant to the topic, thereby nominating themselves for involvement. One member might say, "There is one person with whom I have tried everything. I have tried listening, I have been nondirective, I even have gotten angry a few times, but nothing seems to work." After some additional exploration, the facilitator may ask the member to demonstrate some of the ways in which he or she has responded to the person so that other group members can begin to identify the variety of techniques that are available.

Make the Situation Nonevaluative

The way in which the facilitator leads the discussion will indicate whether or not the focus of the process is on evaluation. A statement such as "Let's see how well people handle this kind of problem" is likely to discourage the participants. A better statement would be "There are probably dozens of ways to respond to this type of issue. It would be helpful to all of us to take a look at three or four different ways of handling the problem and then to begin experimenting with new approaches in order to broaden our range of alternatives." The facilitator can make a wide-ranging statement to establish the idea that role playing is an experimental process rather than an evaluative one. For example: "One of our purposes today is to try handling problems in new ways. We are not concerned with what is the 'right' way but, rather, with experiencing new behaviors and new reactions. Later on, each of you can judge what best fits your own style and situation."

Assign Participants the Roles of Others

Often, the best way of getting started after the warm-up is to ask a group member to play the role of someone with whom he or she interacts. For example, in the case of a teacher who has described a difficult student, the facilitator might ask the teacher to play the role of the student by saying, "You have worked with this student quite a bit; you seem aware of some of his difficulties and sources of resistance. If you could portray the student, it would give other people in the group a chance to work on a similar problem that they may have encountered or may encounter in the future."

Have the Group Define Approaches

Whenever an individual is asked to handle a problem to the best of his or her ability, an element of evaluation and judgment is implied. Other members of the group tend to say, "Here are some things you could have done better" or "I would have handled it differently"—implying that the person did not handle the situation correctly. To avoid this trap, the facilitator can ask the group members to define patterns of behavior and techniques or skills that can be experimented with in a role play. Rather than asking "How would you handle the situation?," the facilitator can summarize or list the various ways of dealing with the problem that have been developed by the group and then ask people to try out those alternatives. In this way, the role player is not necessarily exhibiting what he or she would do but, rather, is trying out an approach or pattern identified by the group to be tested. This changes the emphasis from evaluation to experimentation and selection.

Use Role Rotation

Rather than choosing one person to play the key role and therefore focusing on that individual's skill or lack of it, it often is appropriate to have three or four people handle parts of the role and then discuss the total situation. This avoids direct criticism of one individual and provides linkages between various people who can supplement and complement one another as they experiment with the role-play situation. The facilitator can prepare people for this activity by saying, "Now we are going to try to deal with this troublesome individual. I would like two or three people to try to talk to her and find out what is going on in terms of her resistance. Each person will have two or three minutes. Maybe in the next ten minutes or so, we can find out more about the person and what she is feeling and *then* develop some new strategies for working with her."

Continue the Warm-Up During the Role Play

During the role-play enactment, the connections between the actors and the observers should be maintained. The facilitator can continue the warm-up process by involving group members. For example, one role player might be asked, "Why don't you try to find out a little about how the other person sees things?" The interaction then might proceed for a short period of time, then the facilitator might intervene again to involve the audience: "Most of you have worked with people who are resistant (or whatever the problem is). Does this person sound typical up to now?" Through this intervention, the facilitator takes the focus away from evaluation of the role players and puts it on the type of interaction being presented and the nature of the problem.

The facilitator may then use a wide range of techniques (which are discussed in more detail in Chapter 5) to maintain connections between the role players and the rest of the group members. Role playing is effective when the observers feel that they, too, are represented in front of the room (rather than merely sitting in judgment on someone else's performance). Similarly, the participants who are involved in the enactment are more apt to learn and become more open and spontaneous when they feel that they are part of the group (rather than actors who are about to hear critical reviews from a psychologically distant audience).

Use Action Methods

Role playing facilitates learning through interaction. Once the participants have been assigned roles, it is important to move quickly into enactment. Background information should be minimized at this point; "action" situations are called for.

Developmental role playing is relatively spontaneous and creative. At some point the facilitator may want to stop the action to interview the key role player in order to find out more about how that person is feeling and then to check with the members of the audience (the observers) to determine whether they have shared some of these feelings. At other times, if the audience is supportive and the role players are becoming free and spontaneous, the facilitator may let the role play run for a while and then move into post-enactment discussion. The facilitator also can choose to have people reverse or rotate roles or can direct new people to act out the situation. As many as three or four people can be asked at various times to play the role of the manager/instructor/salesman/counselor while three or four others play role of the subordinate/student/client. A large group can be divided into smaller role-playing groups so that more members can try role playing in a less threatening situation.

As participants become more involved in the process, it may be desirable to summarize principles, techniques, or key ideas that will be useful to the group as it enters the discussion phases of the experiential learning cycle.

Feedback

Because developmental role plays are unstructured, feedback is not specifically built into the process. Just as is the case with the earlier phases of the process, the feedback and post-enactment phase emerges from the group's interests and concerns. Rather than telling the group members what to look for, the facilitator in a developmental session might ask, "At what point did you feel most involved in the process?," "What was most interesting or stimulating to you?," "In what ways were you able to identify with role player A as she responded to the other individual?" In this way, group members may be stimulated to give feedback, but rather than analyzing and evaluating the performances of others, they concentrate on their own empathy and concerns and identify with other members of the group who have been involved in the problem situation.

Summary

Role playing is one of the most exciting techniques available to the trainer in HRD work. It is particularly effective as a training intervention in attempting to solve problems in communication or human interactions because it allows the participants to:

1. Identify the problem;
2. Explore the attitudes and behaviors that contribute to the problem;
3. Develop alternative strategies and behaviors for changing the situation or solving the problem;
4. Receive timely, constructive, descriptive feedback on their behavior;
5. Practice one or more alternative behaviors and refine and repractice until it feels right; and
6. Receive encouragement and/or reinforcement for engaging in an effort to change for the better.

Because role playing is active learning, it requires detailed planning for both content and logistics, and because it is not a "show," it necessitates care in processing, or talking through, the experience before crystallizing its learning. The role-play process allows participants to share their reactions, identify patterns, discuss general principles and generalize from those principles, and plan how they will apply their new learnings and practice new behaviors. Most importantly, role playing creates practical, transferable learning that participants "own" and are likely to apply in their everyday lives.

Role-Play Techniques

Certain techniques can be used in many types of training sessions either to move the group toward predetermined or agreed-on goals or to contribute to the discovery and exploration of new objectives and new modes of behavior. These techniques can be written into structured role plays or can be introduced spontaneously into structured or developmental role plays.

Unstructured or Developmental Techniques

The techniques in this section usually are used in unstructured/developmental role plays. In each case, the specific technique to be used should be a response to the dynamics of the situation and the facilitator's objective in intervening.

Straight or Demonstration Role Playing

In the most common and frequent application of developmental role playing, two individuals are asked to enact a specific scene or situation that is relevant to the defined purposes of the session or to the emerging needs and interests of the participants. A variety of warm-up techniques can be used: asking members to identify key problems in the area under examination; using a videotape or other presentation to elicit involvement; and so on.

The facilitator might state the general topic to be explored in the session and say that he or she would like several participants to demonstrate what a typical problem in that area looks and sounds like so that the group can begin to explore various ways of dealing with it. The facilitator then can ask for examples of the problem, check for commonality of concern, and choose the situation as a point of departure for further examination. "This example will give us a chance to look at the nature of. . .and some of the problems we encounter in that area." The person who provided the example can be asked to play himself or herself and to select another group member to play the part of the other person. The first member then takes the second person to a secluded part of room (or to another room) and briefs him or her on the situation, describing *in general* the behavior of the other person in the example. When they return, the facilitator asks specific questions of the first participant to structure the session: "Where were you when this happened?," "What time was it?," "What was the general atmosphere?," "What were you feeling?," and so on. The two role players then interact.

The facilitator may let the interaction run for a while, or may ask other people to demonstrate similar interactions, or may begin working with the group to develop criteria or strategies for dealing with the situation. The facilitator also may use a variety of techniques to contribute to the spontaneity and insight of the role players. One such technique is called "soliloquizing" or the "on-the-spot interview."

Soliloquizing: The On-the-Spot Interview

The purpose of this technique is to expose more clearly to all participants and observers what is going on in the situation (Is it realistic? Do the people involved understand each other's feelings? Are there other ways in which they could become more clear and more direct?).

As the interaction begins to warm up, to take on a pattern, the facilitator may interrupt in order to validate the reality of the situation and/or to aid group members in developing more insight into what has occurred. The facilitator can ask the primary role player (the one who supplied the example around which the interaction is built), "Is this pretty much the way it happened?" Then, "Tell me how you are feeling now as you begin to try to. . . . Tell me more about that." As the role player's feelings and perceptions become clearer, the facilitator can explore those feelings and what actions are taken based on those feelings. This raises questions about how the individual deals with his or her own anger, confusion, hostility, etc., and whether the role player stays in touch with the second person or begins to alienate the other and create tensions. Alternatively, the facilitator might ask for support and reinforcement for the role player from the observers. "How many of you feel angry and upset when. . . .?"

This interruption of the role play is only temporary and is intended to ensure that the lead participant feels as though the situation is realistic, not simply a charade. It also provides an opportunity for all members of the group to identify with the lead role player and to obtain more insight into the feelings and reactions that occur in handling a situation of this type. Finally, the soliloquy or on-the-spot interview gives the facilitator a chance to introduce alternative approaches. For example, the facilitator might say, "What are some of the other ways in which you might draw this person out?," and then encourage the role players to experiment with them.

Often it is appropriate to let the role play run for a while until the role players become further involved. On the other hand, if involvement is slow in coming, it may be necessary to interrupt and interview one or both of the role players in order to bring the situation into a clear focus and to ensure that participants and observers understand the real issues. If there is lack of clarity, or if the participants do not seem to be "warming up" well, it often is useful to use a technique called "role reversal" or "switching."

Role Reversal

In some situations, the facilitator may ask one role player to change positions with and take on the role previously being played by the other. It is important to actually have the participants change positions; the physical change encourages their mental or psychological change and also keeps the roles clear to those who are observing.

Role reversal accomplishes one or more of the following objectives:

- *Clarifying the situation.* In demonstration role playing, this allows the observers to see how the second person behaved in the *actual* situation through the eyes of the person who supplied the example. It also gives each role player a chance to clarify the facts, to be specific in voicing complaints, and to mirror what he or she perceives to be the attitude of the other.

- *Increasing spontaneity.* Role reversal can help to keep people moving and loose. People who are "stuck" in their usual roles—behaving in stereotyped or mechanical fashion—are shaken out of their stereotypes through role reversal. They are forced to re-examine what is going on from a different perspective and to try out different behavior.

- *Increasing insight and awareness.* Often a simple role reversal makes one or both of the role players more aware of the position of the other person, and the subsequent enactment brings to light some of the feelings and behaviors that might not have been identified otherwise.

The role-reversal technique can be used in combination with on-the-spot interviews to clarify the facts in the situation and to increase insight and spontaneity. For example, when asked whether the second person is representing the other role accurately, the person who described the situation (the lead role player) might say, "No, the real person was much more belligerent than that." The facilitator then could have the role players exchange seats and instruct the lead role player to take the other person's role and to demonstrate how the real person actually behaved. In the meantime, the second role player is instructed to play the lead person's role *as that person has been playing it.* This allows the first role player to see how he or she has been responding to the other and how he or she has been handling the situation. This also allows the role players to gain insight into each other's feelings and motives. When this happens, it usually is productive to have them resume their original roles, pick up a few lines before the spot at which they left off, and continue the role play. Often, the role players will try new approaches.

Role reversal or switching is one of the most powerful role-play techniques. By moving from role to role in various situations, group members increase their flexibility, their awareness of a wider range of attitudes, and their responses and concerns; in general, they enhance their ability to interact more freely and openly within changing situations.

Doubling

A supplemental technique similar to soliloquy is the one introduced in Chapter 3: the use of the "alter ego," often called "doubling." In this case, a third individual is brought into the role-play situation and is asked to become the "inner voice" of one of the role players. The facilitator introduces the idea by saying that when a person is involved in interactions with others, there often are a lot of things in that person's mind that he or she does not care to express or does not have time to express. Our minds work much faster than our words can convey. Therefore, another person will be added to the role play to express the unexpressed thoughts and feelings of one of the role players.

This technique requires quite a bit of direction and prodding from the facilitator because it is new to the participants and they frequently do not understand it at first. One option in this instance is for the facilitator to assume the doubling role the first time in order to demonstrate how it works. A second option is for the facilitator periodically to interrupt the interaction to *interview* the "inner voice" of one of the major role players. By asking pertinent questions and encouraging the double to soliloquize, the facilitator can call attention to some positive actions that possibly could be taken.

A variation of this technique is a representation of contemplation. The role player states his or her position and feelings about the situation, then the double thinks along with the role player, out loud. The role player is instructed to correct the double if that person goes off track. If the role player agrees with what the double is saying, he or she is to continue or extend the thought. In this way, the person is almost having a conversation with himself or herself. Thoughts are clarified and extended; ideas are explored; actions are considered, and so on. In some cases, the technique results in the two representives of the person spurring each other on and becoming "stirred up" about new thoughts and new possibilities.

There are many possible applications of this technique. It can be used to warm up role players. It is quite useful in demonstrating how a salesperson gets ready to make a call or how a lawyer gets ready to present a case. It also can be used in a slightly different form called "group doubling."

Group Doubling

In this technique, the entire group or portions of the group are asked to express the inner, or unexpressed, thoughts or feelings of one or more role players. For example, if two instructors have just demonstrated a disciplinary interaction between a manager and an employee, the facilitator will divide the group in half so that half the participants serve as the "double" for the manager and the other half double for the employee. The facilitator would invite the "managers" to express some of their feelings and reactions to the employee as a result of the discussion they just held. It is all right if this turns into a little bit of a free-for-all; more than one "manager" may be talking at once, and there may be some interrupting and some "piggybacking." This session is intended to surface emotions, to get ideas and feelings out into the open. After the manager's doubles have expressed their opinions, the facilitator asks to hear how the employee's doubles feel.

On some occasions, this technique can be turned back into straight role playing by having one of the employee's doubles and one of the manager's doubles continue the discussion in front of the group. The emotion of the real-life situation can be validated and strengthened by the doubling process.

Tag Teams

In this variation of the alter ego/doubling technique, two people are assigned the same role. As the role play begins, one of the two members begins playing the role and continues to do so until he or she becomes "stuck." Then, using a prearranged, *nonverbal* signal such as a touch on the shoulder (tag), the first player asks the second to step in and take over the role. The second person then plays the role as long as progress is being made. Conversely, if the first player is having difficulty in dealing with a problem in the role play, and the second player thinks that he or she has a solution, the second person may use the signal, asking the first role player to let him or her have a chance. Tag-team pairs can agree prior to the role play on what signal they will use and when (in what circumstances) a transfer of role would be in order. The post-role play processing then would include a discussion between the members of the tag team. If managed properly, this discussion can lead to clarification of the situation and the behaviors of role players, clarification of the tag-team's role and the way it might be approached, identification of alternatives, and increased understanding and bonding between the tag-team pairs.

Mirroring

In the mirror technique, rather than speaking as the inner voice of the role player, the second person takes on the role of the other and portrays it *as the first person is playing it*, to "mirror back" to the role player how he or she appears.

The second application of the mirror technique is used to engage people in role playing who are hesitant about or resistant to becoming involved. For example, participant A may talk quite a bit about how she would handle a difficult colleague but, when asked to demonstrate her approach, she resists. The facilitator might say, "Since member A would rather not portray the role of the person who is dealing with the. . .co-worker, perhaps someone else will play the role as A has described it. Member A, is that all right with you?" Participants almost always agree to let someone else play their roles, at least early in the session. The facilitator then can call on someone to take the role of A, and A is encouraged to suggest ways in which the situation could be handled differently. Thus, role player A becomes involved and may interrupt the role-play interaction to suggest different ways of behaving. It is not at all unusual for member A finally to volunteer to demonstrate some of her ideas within a role play.

There are other variations of mirroring. After small-group discussion or confrontation, members of the group can be asked to portray one another. Everyone changes roles: A becomes B, B becomes C, and so on. A simpler version of the technique is to ask two or three people to show another person how that person has acted in a given situation by mirroring the person's behavior. If only one person is singled out to be mirrored, it can be embarrassing and evoke tension. However, in the spontaneous role play, if from time to time different individuals are asked to mirror back to others, the technique can gain acceptance in the group and become a way of communicating perceptions and feelings without attacks or negative feedback. In two techniques to be described later—behavior rehearsal and behavior modeling—participants can learn how to portray a role more effectively by mirroring a more experienced person or a filmed presentation of an appropriate procedure or style.

Empty Chair

In Gestalt therapy, developed by Fritz Perls, there is an experiment called "dialog" or "open chair," in which an individual engages in a dialog between two different aspects of himself or herself or with another person who is not there. The individual moves from one chair to another to indicate movement from the one person or aspect to the other. This technique can be applied effectively to role playing.

At times, a group member may have difficulty interacting with another person because the member is so preoccupied with trying to relate to and impress that other person. The group member can be relieved of the pressure of having to deal with the specific person by having an empty chair be used to simulate the other person. The member does not have to be concerned about how the chair responds. At the same time, he or she can gain the experience of trying to deal with the other person.

Often the empty-chair technique leads to other interactions in which someone is asked to move into the chair and portray the symbolic role that has not yet been revealed. Or the group member who is experiencing the problem may choose to move into the chair. This leads to the technique that follows.

Self-Role Play or Monodrama

An individual often can gain insight into a given interaction by playing both roles, by literally switching between two chairs. Thus, for example, the individual plays the role of the supervisor, says what he or she has to say (or believes the supervisor would say) in that role, and then shifts to the role of the subordinate by moving to the other chair. As the subordinate, the person answers the supervisor and then returns to the supervisor's chair again to continue the exchange. It takes some experience and practice to make this technique effective, but it is widely used in developmental role playing and, with some experimentation, can be very useful.

Shifting Physical Position

Communication problems or relationships can be dramatized by changing physical positions. In one example, the person playing the part of a dissatisfied customer will gradually turn her back to the person playing the salesperson to indicate the opinion that the salesperson is not truly listening to her objection or complaint. Another variation is to have one individual stand while the other remains seated in order to dramatize a hierarchical or authoritarian relationship. The facilitator can interview the person who is seated, asking, "What is your reaction to having. . .standing and looking down at you?" Other variations of this technique include moving chairs farther apart or closer together and having group members shake hands or make physical contact during an interaction.

Role Rotation

At times it is useful to move a series of people quickly through one role. For example, an individual may be asked to play the part of an angry citizen talking to a public official. Those being trained to be more effective in the role of public official can be asked in sequence to move into that role as the angry citizen continually makes the same complaint. In a very brief time, ten or fifteen people can experience the role and give a one- or two-sentence response to the angry citizen.

This technique has two purposes. One is to elicit a wide range of responses; people can compare approaches and develop new awareness of the range of possibilities available to them. Second, role rotation often is a useful warm-up technique, allowing people to try new approaches and experiment with new behavior.

On-the-Spot Inventions

In developmental role playing, where there is no predetermined structure and system, it often is possible and useful for the facilitator and group members to improvise new ways of gaining insight or improving skills. For example, if an individual in the group is having trouble being firm or assertive with a resistant person, the facilitator might ask the group to suggest experiments that the individual could try in order to come across more forcefully. Someone might say, "Why don't you try pointing your finger at the person? I'm not suggesting that you do this all the time, but it might give you a feeling of firmness or resolve." Someone else might suggest, "Why don't you try leaning forward a little bit? You seem to be rocking back on your heels." In an open, spontaneous session, people find ways of assisting one another to learn, to experiment, to explore their own potential, and to develop their own resources.

In summary, there is a wide range of unstructured techniques, some of which have been used in many situations over a long period of time: role reversal, doubling, and the mirror technique are three. Many other techniques emerge as the facilitator and group members search for new ways of relating to one another and new ways of solving problems and producing results.

Structured Techniques

Structured role playing has been defined as role playing in which there are predetermined objectives and in which roles, background information, and procedures have, for the most part, been planned and designed prior to the session. One of the characteristics of the structured approach to role playing is that it does not rely on spontaneous interventions. Many role plays can be conducted by relatively inexperienced trainers, and many designs are utilized by educational groups, voluntary agencies, industrial organizations, and various other groups without employing HRD professionals. In addition, structured role plays often are part of larger programs that include other training technologies such as structured experiences, instruments, lecturettes, simulations, small-group discussions, and so on.

The techniques that facilitate and energize this type of role playing are quite different from those used in developmental sessions. Although it is possible to include a role reversal or the mirror technique, these would be unusual interventions in the structured role-play process.

Multiple-Group Role Playing

As has been discussed previously, in multiple-group role playing, several small groups are provided with the same role-play assignment and they act out the situation simultaneously. In most instances, the process is programed: specific objectives are defined; time frames are indicated; and formats are used to elicit specific aras of concern and to provide a common focus for discussion.

Built-In Tension

Whether a role play is conducted as a demonstration or in a multiple format, the core of the structured approach is in the design itself and, therefore, often is difficult to identify. The energizing force in making structured role plays work is *built-in tension*. For example, if managers are being trained in performance-review techniques and are asked to role play an appraisal interview, the role-play design is not likely to be useful or successful if it does not include areas of disagreement or tension. There are several types of tension or conflict-building devices that can be used in designing a structured role play.

Conflict or Contradiction in Information

People can be given conflicting background or role information to create tension. However, this information must be realistic and resolvable when exposed and explored further. For example, in a performance-appraisal role play the subordinate might be instructed: "You have had quite a few complaints from customers lately. The basic cause of these complaints is a new system that was installed by the engineering staff. The system is experimental, and although your boss was told about this, she was never given the specifics of the new approach. You have done all you could to resolve the causes of the complaints. You did not want to put too much pressure on the engineers. You think that your boss would have said something if she had wanted you to take a stand."

Concurrently, the instructions for the supervisor's role might include the following: "You are aware that your subordinate has been receiving a lot of complaints. This in in part because of a new engineering approach. You think that your subordinate should have been more assertive in not letting this approach get out of hand and cause customer dissatisfaction."

Conflicts in Immediate Past Experience

Differences in experience can be built in to roles in order to provide a basis for examining various approaches to solving problems and resolving conflict. For example, role player A (an executive) could be told that he or she has always found a certain worker to be quiet and unassuming, while role player B (the worker's supervisor) could be told that this worker is belligerent and a troublemaker, but that the worker says very little when a member of top management is around. The issue then is not whether one role player is right or wrong about the worker; the issue is what these two role players are trying to achieve, how well they share information, how they solve the problem, and what the results of their discussion are. The content of the conflict is not terribly important; it is the process of resolving it that matters.

Differences in Roles or Responsibilities

Any number of management and organizational problems occur because individuals are loyal to a given group or department. For example, in a university it is not at all unusual for the members of any particular department to have difficulty resolving differences with components of the university outside that department. In a structured role play designed to involve people in interdisciplinary-development activities, the problem could be dramatized by having one role player be a professor of liberal arts and the other play a professor of mathematics. These two are members of a small committee that is trying to work out an interdisciplinary curriculum. The members of the committee generally agree that basic, liberal arts courses should precede any kind of professional or specialized education. The professor of liberal arts further believes that liberal arts should be the major focus in undergraduate years, with students moving on into professional or technical disciplines afterward. The professor of mathematics, on the other hand, does not think that specific liberal arts prerequisites should be built into the curriculum. As far as he or she is concerned, half a dozen or so liberal arts courses *of the student's own choice* are enough. The role play would then be a meeting between these two. To make it more complicated, a few additional committee members, with varying points of view on the subject, could be added to the role-play meeting. A variation of this technique would be to assign role players conflicting responsibilities or concerns.

Differences in Objectives

Conflict can be induced easily in a group situation by providing people with different objectives. For example, in business role plays, tension can be created simply by saying, "Your goal is to maximize the profitability of your unit." The intergroup competition that results provides the basis for much learning.

Built-In Resolution

It is not sufficient simply to build conflict or tension into a structured role play. Opportunities also must be provided for the resolution of that conflict. This is achieved by including explicit or implicit options for resolution.

In their book, *The Role-Play Technique,* Maier, Solem, and Maier (1975) provide many examples of structured role plays with built-in tensions. However if the role players examine the situational context, look for alternatives, and avoid yes-no positions, they can find many opportunities for appropriate solutions. In one case, the authors sum up the objective of the process in a way that is typical of structured role playing:

> *It is apparent that problems stated in situational terms are the most likely to prevent defensive reactions and the most likely to contain a mutual interest. However, interest in problem solving might cause some employees to become critical of others. It is at such time that the leader must protect the individual who is attacked. She can point out that the aim is to solve the problem in a manner suitable to all, that there are bound to be differences in values and viewpoints, and that the purpose of the discussion is to understand and resolve the differences. At all times the leader's job is to keep the discussion situation-oriented and to respect differences in needs, values, and attitudes. (pp. 118-119)*

Summary

Two types of role-play techniques are available to the role-play facilitator. *Developmental or unstructured techniques* are used to facilitate the training group's involvement in an innovative, emerging process of learning. Materials and techniques are not predetermined. Role reversal, soliloquy, doubling, and other action methods can be injected into the role play as it unfolds. *Structured techniques* focus on predetermined goals, training materials, and formats. Multiple role playing often is used to engage group members in concurrent enactments so that principles and relationships can be clarified and skills can be practiced by all members. Structured and unstructured methods can be combined in a series of sessions, or within one session, to provide opportunities for learning through experimentation, discovery, and innovation, as well as through systematic, organized enactments and discussions.

Reference and Bibliography

The *Annual* series for HRD practitioners. (1972, 1973, 1974, 1975, 1976, 1977, 1978, 1979, 1980, 1981, 1982, 1983, 1984, 1985, 1986, 1987, 1988). J.W. Pfeiffer, J.E. Jones, & L.D. Goodstein (Eds.). San Diego, CA: University Associates.

Argyris, C. (1951, May). *Role playing in action.* New York State School of Industrial and Labor Relations, Cornell University. Bulletin No. 16.

Borgatta, E.F. (1956). Analysis of social interaction: Actual, role playing and projective. *Journal of Abnormal and Social Psychology, 40,* 190-196.

Corsini, R.J. (1957, April). *The role playing technique in business and industry.* Chicago: Industrial Relations Center. Occasional Paper No.9.

Corsini, R.J. (1966). *Roleplaying in psychotherapy: A manual.* Chicago: Aldine.

French, J.R.P. (1945). Role playing as a method of training foremen. *Sociometry, 8,* 410-422.

A handbook of structured experiences for human relations training (Vols. I through X). (1969, 1970, 1971, 1973, 1975, 1977, 1979, 1981, 1983, 1985). J.W. Pfeiffer & J.E. Jones (Eds.). San Diego, CA: University Associates.

Hanson, P.G. (1975). Giving feedback: An interpersonal skill. In J.E. Jones & J.W. Pfeiffer (Eds.), *The 1975 annual handbook for group facilitators.* San Diego, CA: University Associates.

Hanson, P.G. (1981). *Learning through groups: A trainer's basic guide* (Chapter 3: Feedback in training groups). San Diego, CA: University Associates.

Lippitt, R. (1943). The psychodrama in leadership training. *Sociometry, 6,* 286-292.

Maier, N.R.F. (1952). *Principles of Human Relations: Applications to Management.* New York: John Wiley.

Maier, N.R.F. (1953). Dramatized case material as a springboard for role playing. *Group Psychotherapy, 6,* 30-42.

Maier, N.R.F. (1973). *Psychology in industrial organizations* (4th ed.). Boston: Houghton Mifflin.

Maier, N.R.F., Solem, A.R., & Maier, A.A. (1975). *The role-play technique: A handbook for management and leadership practice.* San Diego, CA: University Associates.

Moreno, J.L. (1923). *Das Stegreif Theater.* Potsdam: Kiepenhever.

Shaw, M.E., Corsini, R.J., Blake, R.R., & Mouton, J.S. (1980). *Role playing: A practical manual for group facilitators.* San Diego, CA: University Associates.

Starr, A. (1977). *Rehearsal for living: Psychodrama.* Chicago: Nelson-Hall.

Appendix 1:
Sources of UA Role Plays

Numerous role plays have been published in the form of structured experiences in the University Associates *Handbook* and *Annual* series, and these can be used as guides in developing others. Most of the activities listed below are role plays; the others are "quasi-role plays," i.e., activities that have a role-play component although, in some cases, individual participants are not assigned specific roles.

Handbooks
- "Committee Meeting: Demonstrating Hidden Agendas," in Volume I of the *Handbook*;
- "Choosing a Color: A Multiple Role Play," Volume I, *Handbook*;
- "Wahoo City: A Role Alternation," Volume III, *Handbook*;
- "Pine County: Information Sharing in a Task Group," Volume IV, *Handbook*;
- "Staff Meeting: A Leadership Role Play," Volume VI, *Handbook*;
- "HELPCO: An OD Role Play," Volume VI, *Handbook*;
- "Power Personalities: A Role Play," Volume VII, *Handbook*;
- "Sexual Values in Organizations: An OD Role Play," Volume VII, *Handbook*;
- "Sunglow: An Appraisal Role Play," Volume VII, *Handbook*;
- "Organizational TA: Interpersonal Communication," Volume VIII, *Handbook*;

- "Elm Street Community Church: Third-Party Consultation," Volume IX, *Handbook*;
- "Ajax Appliance Corporation: Exploring Conflict-Management Styles," Volume X, *Handbook*.

Annuals

- "Energy International: A Problem-Solving Multiple Role Play," in the 1972 *Annual*;
- "Strategies of Changing: A Multiple Role Play," 1973 *Annual*;
- "Roxboro Electric Company: An OD Role Play," 1974 *Annual*;
- "Live Case: A Group Diagnosis," 1975 *Annual*;
- "Lindell-Billings Corporation: A Confrontation Role Play," 1975 *Annual*;
- "Faculty Meeting: A Multiple Role Play," 1977 *Annual*;
- "Tri-State: A Multiple Role Play," 1977 *Annual*;
- "Admissions Committee: A Consensus-Seeking Activity," 1978 *Annual*;
- "Balance of Power: A Cooperation/Competition Activity," 1978 *Annual*;
- "Defensive and Supportive Communication: A Dyadic Role Play," 1979 *Annual*;
- "Choosing an Apartment: Authority Issues in Groups," 1980 *Annual*;
- "Missiles: Sources of Stress," 1980 *Annual*;
- "Power and Affiliation: A Role Play," 1980 *Annual*;
- "Move to Newtown: A Collaboration Activity," 1980 *Annual*;
- "Budget Cutting: Conflict and Consensus Seeking," 1982 *Annual*;
- "Assistant Wanted: An Employment Interview," 1983 *Annual*;
- "Conflict Role Play: Resolving Differences," 1983 *Annual*;
- "Inquiries and Discoveries: Managing Interviewing Situations," 1984 *Annual*;
- "Role Power: Understanding Influence," 1984 *Annual*;
- "Trouble in Manufacturing: Managing Interpersonal Conflict," 1984 *Annual*;

- "Datatrak: Dealing with Organizational Conflict," 1984 *Annual*;
- "Management Perspectives: Identifying Styles," 1985 *Annual*;
- "Performance Appraisal: A Practice Session," 1987 *Annual*;
- "Society of Taos: Group Decision Making," 1987 *Annual*;
- "Winterset High School: An Intergroup-Conflict Simulation," 1987 *Annual*;
- "Understanding the Need for Approval: Toward Personal Autonomy," 1988 *Annual*;
- "The VMX Productions, Inc.: Handling Resistance Positively," 1988 *Annual*.

Appendix 2:
Sample Role Play

The New Truck Dilemma

Norman R.F. Maier, Allen R. Solem,
and Ayesha A. Maier

Focusing the Problem

Whenever people are involved in a joint activity, the question of fair treatment becomes an important issue about which opinions differ. Although a supervisor may try to be fair, he soon realizes that no amount of effort on his part to do the right thing is appreciated by everyone. Consequently, he often welcomes rules and company practices, because they promise to protect him from the charge of playing favorites. These same rules and formalized procedures may be regarded by employees as arbitrary, inconvenient, and a way of disregarding individual differences in needs; yet employees prefer them to favoritism, which they believe will occur if supervisory judgments prevail. Management sees rules and formalized procedures as necessary evils that interfere with flexibility and personalized practices. However, these procedures also serve as guides and protections from complaints and permit the

Reprinted from *The Role-Play Technique: A Handbook for Management and Leadership Practice* by Norman R.F. Maier, Allen R. Solem, and Ayesha A. Maier, 1975, San Diego, CA: University Associates. Copyright © by Allen R. Solem and Ayesha A. Maier. Used with permission.

supervisor to let the blame fall on the rule. Thus, the rule can be attacked by both parties to a dispute.

It is necessary to clarify the issues involved in a dispute over fairness. Disagreement on issues of fairness may be unavoidable because choices and preferences are, by their very nature, self-centered. It is apparent that if all members of a group had an equal desire for an object, regardless of whether each had an equal claim to it, there would be a struggle since each would try to get it for himself. An outsider might, however, work out a just solution by dividing it equally between members of the group. When an object can be shared or divided, opportunities for finding fair solutions exist, providing that each member respects the claims of others. When, however, needs and claims differ among group members and an object cannot be shared, the difficulties mount.

Some of the more common fairness issues include the following situations:

- How can vacations be scheduled more fairly?
- Who gets time off during hunting seasons?
- What is a fair division of overtime?
- Who should do a disagreeable job?
- Which unit should try out the new chairs?
- Which group should get more space as a result of a move to new quarters?
- How can office space be allocated so that some are not left with less space or less elegant furnishings than others?

Frequently, supervisors are unaware of the many factors that play a part in a dispute about fairness. As the previous list of problems shows, prestige is an issue, and when social recognition is part of the problem of fairness, the emotional involvement is strong.

The incident in this case hinges on the issuing of a new truck to one member of a crew of workers, each of whom uses a truck in his work. The foreman finds himself in a situation in which he must make a wise and fair decision. Since the replacement of trucks has been infrequent, the importance of making the right decision is apparent to the foreman.

The multiple role-playing procedure is used in this case because it is desirable to obtain solutions from a number of groups.

Multiple Role-Playing Procedure

Preparation

1. The participants form groups of six persons each. If the last group has only five persons, they may assume that one of them (George) is home because of illness. Less than five persons may act as observers of role-playing groups.
2. All participants read the General Instructions for Role Players. This data may be consulted during the role play. The instructor may wish to post on newsprint the facts about the repairmen and their trucks.
3. Each group selects one member to play the foreman, Walt Marshall.
4. Other group members play George, Bill, John, Charlie, and Hank. If a group has only five persons, the foreman reads George's role and assumes that he has talked to George on the telephone.
5. The member of each group playing the foreman studies his role sheet. When he has read it, he stands up to indicate to the instructor that he is ready to role play.
6. Crew members study their role sheets. They avoid reading other roles or discussing the roles with one another.
7. The observers (if any) read their instructions in preparation for their observation of the role play.
8. Each crew member writes his role name on a slip of paper which he wears as a name tag so that other members know who he is.
9. The crew members assume they are in the foreman's office waiting for him.
10. When all participants who are playing the part of the foreman have indicated by standing that they are ready to begin role playing, the instructor asks them to sit down. This signals that the foremen have entered their offices to begin the discussions.
11. Crew members greet the foreman on his arrival, and the role play begins.

Process

1. Groups need between twenty-five and thirty minutes for role playing. Those who have not finished at the end of twenty-eight minutes are given a two-minute warning signal.
2. During the role play, the instructor lists on newsprint the appropriate headings for the recording of solutions and other results from the groups. Sample Table 1 illustrates the types of headings and the method for recording data that may be used. The first letter of each crew member's name is arranged in a column. One column is needed for each group. Arrows may be used to indicate any exchange in trucks. (These should be added later.) An arrow from the left pointing to a name indicates the man who got the new truck, while other arrows (to the right of names) indicate who got his truck, etc. For example, in Group 3, John receives the new truck while Charlie gets John's truck, and Charlie's truck is to be discarded. (This is not a typical solution.)
3. In addition to making arrangements for recording the exchange in trucks, the instructor should plan space for other data. Suggested headings are given below:
   a. "Repairs" indicates whose truck, if any, will be fixed up in any way.
   b. "Number of Exchanges" serves to record the number of men who benefit by the fact that a new truck is introduced into the crew. In Group 3, shown in the sample table, both John and Charlie receive different trucks as a result of the solution.
   c. The heading "Foreman Satisfied" is used to indicate whether the foreman is satisfied or not with the solution reached in the discussion.
   d. A fourth heading, "Dissatisfied Drivers," is used to record the initials of the men who are not satisfied with the outcome.

Collecting Group Data

1. The foreman for each group reports (a) the decision for his group, by indicating the name of the man who gets the new truck, the disposition that is made of his truck, etc.; (b) whose

truck, if any, is to be repaired; and (c) whether or not he is satisfied with the outcome.

2. The instructor diagrams the solution as the foreman reports it, and fills in lines (a), (b), and (c) of the table.

3. The crew criticizes the foreman's report if they see fit, and all who are dissatisfied give their reasons—to be reported on line (d) of the table.

4. Observers, if used, briefly report on the discussion process each observed, commenting especially on (a) how the foreman presented the problem, (b) how the crew responded in the discussion, and (c) any helpful or interfering things the foreman did.

5. The process is repeated until all groups have reported. If more than twelve groups participate, it may be necessary to limit complete reports to ten groups and request the remaining groups to confine their reports to the presentation of their solutions.

General Discussion

All participants then discuss such topics as the following:

1. In what ways are the solutions alike or different?

2. Which of the several solutions is best? (The percentage of satisfied individuals is determined.)

3. What factors influenced differences of opinion on the "best" solution?

4. Could a foreman have made a fair decision on this problem? How many members in a group could he please?

5. What sets of values enter into the question of fairness? (The arguments used by various individuals are listed on newsprint.)

6. Could a company write a rule for the fair way to distribute the new trucks?

7. What solutions would be unacceptable to management? Were any such solutions suggested by groups and, if so, could they have been prevented?

8. Can the problem of fairness be settled by a discussion with the crew without the foreman attempting to influence the outcome? (Arguments for and against this position are listed in separate columns.)

9. In the opinion of each crew member, what did he like most about the foreman's conduct of the meeting, and what did he like least about it? (The instructor may make a two-column listing of these behaviors. Key words should be used to characterize a behavioral item, and check marks may be made to register duplicate contributions. Discuss various interpretations of the two lists.)

10. What other problems are basically like the new truck problem? (The instructor lists these on newsprint. In cases of disagreement, differences in opinion are indicated by means of a modifying phrase.)

General Instructions for Role Players[1]

You work for the telephone company, and one of you is the foreman while the others are repairmen. The job of a repairman is to fix phones that are out of order, and it requires knowledge and diagnostic skills as well as muscular skills. Repairmen must climb telephone poles, work with small tools, and meet customers. The foreman of a crew is usually an ex-repairman; this happens to be true in this case. He has an office at the garage location but spends a good deal of time making the rounds, visiting the places where the men are working. Each repairman works alone and ordinarily does several jobs in a day. The foreman gives help and instruction as needed.

The repairmen drive to various locations in the city to do repair work. Each of them drives a small truck and takes pride in its appearance. The repairmen have possessive feelings about their trucks and like to keep them in good running order. Naturally, they like to have new trucks, because new trucks give them a feeling of pride.

Here are some facts about the repairmen and their trucks.

	Years With Company	Type of Truck Used
George	17	2-year-old Ford
Bill	11	5-year-old Dodge
John	10	4-year-old Ford
Charlie	5	3-year-old Ford
Hank	3	5-year-old Chevrolet

Most of the men do all their driving in the city, but John and Charlie cover the jobs in the suburbs.

In playing your part, accept the facts as given and assume the attitude supplied in your specific role. From this point on, let your feelings develop in accordance with the events that occur during the role play. When facts or events arise that are not covered by the roles, make up things that are consistent with the way it might be in a real-life situation.

---

[1]Role instructions are taken from an article by N.R.F. Maier and L.F. Zerfoss, "MRP: A Technique for Training Large Groups of Supervisors and Its Potential Use in Social Research," *Human Relations*, 1952, *5*, 180-181. Permission to reproduce the roles has been granted by the Plenum Publishing Company, London, England.

Role Sheet: Walt Marshall, Foreman

You are the foreman of a crew of repairmen, each of whom drives a small service truck to and from his various jobs. Every so often, you get a new truck to exchange for an old one and you have the problem of deciding which of your men should have the new truck. Often there are hard feelings, because each man seems to feel he is entitled to the new truck, so you have a tough time being fair. As a matter of fact, it usually turns out that whatever you decide, most of the men consider it wrong. You now have to face the same issue again because a new Chevrolet truck has just been allocated to you for distribution.

In order to handle this problem, you have decided to put the question to the men themselves. You will tell them about the new truck and ask them what is the fairest way to distribute the trucks. Do not take a position yourself because you want to do what the men think is fair.

Role Sheet: George, Repairman

When a new Chevrolet truck becomes available, you think you should get it because you have the most seniority and don't like your present truck. Your own car is a Chevrolet and you prefer a Chevrolet truck such as you drove before you got the Ford.

Role Sheet: Bill, Repairman

You think you deserve a new truck; it certainly is your turn. Your present truck is old, and since the more senior man has a fairly new truck, you should get the next one. You have taken excellent care of your present Dodge and have kept it looking like new. A man deserves to be rewarded if he treats the company truck like his own.

Role Sheet: John, Repairman

You have to do more driving than most of the other men because you work in the suburbs. You have a fairly old truck and you think you should have the new one because you do so much driving.

Role Sheet: Charlie, Repairman

The heater in your present truck is inadequate. Since Hank backed into the door of your truck, it has never been repaired correctly. The door lets in too much cold air and you attribute your frequent colds to this. You want to have a warm truck since you have a good deal of driving to do. As long as it has good tires and brakes and is comfortable, you don't care about its make.

Role Sheet: Hank, Repairman

You have the worst truck in the crew. It is five years old and had been in a bad wreck before you got it. It has never been good, and you have put up with it for three years. It's about time you got a good truck to drive and it seems only fair that the next one should be yours. You have had only one accident. That was when you sprung the door of Charlie's truck as he opened it when you were backing out of the garage. You hope the new truck is a Ford, since you prefer to drive that make.

Observer Instruction Sheet

Using the following items as a guide, note what the foreman does and how the crew reacts.

1. How did the foreman present the problem?
   a. In presenting the problem, did he display the attitude of asking for help?
   b. Did he present all the facts?
   c. Was his presentation of the problem brief and to the point?
   d. Did he avoid suggesting a solution?
2. What things occurred in the discussion?
   a. Did all group members participate?
   b. Was there free exchange of feelings between group members?
   c. Did the group use social pressure to influence any of its members?
   d. On which member of the crew was social pressure used?
   e. Was the foreman permissive?
   f. Did the foreman avoid taking sides or favoring any person?
   g. What were the points of disagreement in the group?
3. What did the foreman do to help solve the problem?
   a. Did he ask questions to help the group explore ideas?
   b. Did he accept all ideas equally?
   c. Did he avoid hurrying the group to develop a solution?
   d. Did he avoid favoring any solution?
   e. Who supplied the final solution?
   f. What did the foreman do, if anything, to get a consensus on the final solution?

Sample Table 1. Results of New Truck Problem

	Group 1	Group 2	Group 3	Group 4	Group 5
Group Solution Reached	G B J C H	G B J C H	G B J C H	G B J C H	G B J C H
a. Repairs	C	*No*	C	C, J, H	B
b. Number of Exchanges	1	4	2	1	2
c. Foreman Satisfied	*Yes*	*Yes*	*No*	*No*	*Yes*
d. Dissatisfied Drivers	G, B, J	0	G, H	G	J, C

Comments and Implications

This case usually results in an experience of success for the participants. Because most persons who play the part of the foreman have no preconceived solution in mind, they do little talking and are content to sit back and listen. The importance of this state of mind in the foreman can be demonstrated dramatically by asking a person who is to play the foreman to commit himself ahead of time on a solution that he considers to be fair. Such foremen have a difficult time and are inclined to think that the crew is unreasonable. When, however, the crew members realize that their foreman wants to do what they consider fair, there is a free expression of viewpoints. It soon becomes apparent that the opinions of the crew conflict; the noise level in the room rises during this stage. Often the foreman is overwhelmed by the arguing and wishes he had not consulted the group. Fortunately, however, because he usually does not know what to do, he does not interfere too much.

After all members have stated their position, certain members of the group perceive that the conflict is leading nowhere and begin to search for ways to resolve it. Respect for the rights of others becomes more apparent and constructive suggestions are proposed. The sound level now declines considerably. A solution gradually emerges as differences are resolved and concessions are made.

It is important that the foreman refrain from taking sides or agreeing with certain persons; in so doing, he tends only to antagonize others. Rather, he must continue to be patient and regard the conflict as a problem to be solved. Since most groups reach a decision that leaves few or none dissatisfied, it is apparent that the opportunity to express conflicting opinions can lead to a resolution of conflict. In fact, the airing of different views in a freely led discussion is an essential process in the reaching of an agreement. No amount of explaining by a foreman can accomplish this end.

For those crew members who remain dissatisfied, the cause is frequently something that happened during the discussion. Often, the foreman took sides against them, other members attacked them and the foreman failed to protect them, or the foreman ignored the ideas they expressed.

Less than completely satisfactory solutions are caused by a tendency (1) to solve the problem before each member has aired his views fully, and (2) to settle on the first constructive suggestion offered. The foreman can use his status to see that these things do not occur. It is often wise for the foreman to say, "Before we settle on that plan, let's take a look at some other possibilities." It is perhaps too much to expect that all crew members in all groups will be satisfied. Certain employees will create problems. However, as in real life, they usually number less than 10 percent of the total.

Since the issue in this case centers on the question of fairness, and since fairness is a personal matter, the crucial issue is one of employee *acceptance*. The group's decision is perhaps the best way to obtain maximum acceptance, but this does not mean that the foreman should not be concerned with the solution process. He is needed to conduct the discussion and to see that every member has a right to express himself. A point of special interest is the fact that George, the senior man, gets the new truck about half the time—but he gets it more often when he is considerate of others than when he is demanding. Seniority, it seems, is respected, but the senior member's conduct can lower this respect. Since each crew member gets the new truck on occasion, it becomes apparent that the manner in which the men conduct themselves in the discussion is one determinant of the outcome. Although the facts furnished by the role instructions are important, it must not be assumed that they alone should or do determine the solution.

The question of the objective *quality* of the solution does play some part in this case, but the results indicate that it is not a serious problem.

A poor solution is one in which a relatively good truck is discarded. It may be noted from the results obtained that most— if not all—crews reach the decision to discard Hank's truck. This solution conforms with the foreman's view and is therefore acceptable to management. Even though the foreman may not have suggested this solution, it seems that the crew may be depended on to do the right thing. Thus, the fear that a qualitatively poor solution may occur if the crew members make the decision is unrealistic.

It is possible also to argue that solutions that give several people a different truck are superior to those that give a different truck to only one or two. Participants, however, challenge this point and regard it as a matter of preference.

The frequent tendency to repair Charlie's truck is of special interest. Usually the foreman agrees early in the discussion to repair Charlie's truck. Sometimes Charlie does not even keep the truck that is to be repaired. The fact that Charlie exaggerates the condition of his truck because he wants the new one tends to be overlooked. The foreman gives in because he feels that the complaint is a reasonable one and, furthermore, that the request is an inexpensive one—particularly when he finds that everyone else, at this stage of the discussion, is asking for a new truck. It is a common error to take early complaints too seriously. Of course, trucks should be kept in repair, but what constitutes proper repair sometimes is debatable.

How to distribute the new truck is a typical example of the problem of fairness. The values and issues raised in this case are similar to those raised whenever it is impossible to treat all persons alike. If a group decides the matter, the issue is resolved in terms of needs and values existing in the group at that time. Fair solutions must be tailor-made solutions, and no formula can be written that will take all variables into proper consideration. In order to be fair, all persons concerned must be made aware of the needs of others, and participants must discover that fairness cannot be achieved by judging others.

Appendix 3: Guidelines for Giving and Receiving Feedback

Feedback in Training Groups

Philip G. Hanson

Feedback As a Steering Apparatus

The process of giving, asking for, and receiving feedback is probably the most important dimension in training. Indeed, the exchange of feedback is a crucial communication process in any interpersonal relationship. It is through feedback that we can learn "to see ourselves as others see us." Giving or "sending" feedback is a verbal or nonverbal process through which we let others know our perceptions and feelings about *their* behavior. When *soliciting* feedback, an individual is asking for others' perceptions and feelings about his or her own behavior.

Reprinted from Chapter 3, "Feedback in Training Groups," in *Learning Through Groups: A Trainer's Basic Guide* by Philip G. Hanson, 1981, San Diego, CA: University Associates.

Feedback as a means of exchanging personal impressions and reactions seldom is used intentionally in everyday social interactions and, when used, seldom is effective in providing a learning experience for the recipient. In the training environment, however, feedback can be exchanged in relative safety; it is the primary method by which participants develop more effective ways to monitor and assess the impact of their ongoing interactions. In an atmosphere in which choice of one's behavior and ownership of that behavior are stressed, participants can use feedback to help them make choices about changing or not changing their behavior and to test whether or not attempted changes actually are achieved.

The term "feedback" was borrowed from rocket engineering by Kurt Lewin (1947, 1951), a founder of laboratory education. A rocket sent into space contains a mechanism that sends signals back to Earth. A steering apparatus on Earth receives these signals, makes adjustments if the rocket is off target, and corrects the course. Within the training group, members can perform the function of the steering apparatus for each other by sending signals to members who are off target in terms of the learning goals they have set for themselves.

It is not easy to give feedback so that it can be accepted without threat by another individual. To master the technique, one must have courage, sensitivity to other people's needs, and the ability to put oneself in another's shoes. In the training environment, emphasis is placed on developing attitudes of caring, trust, acceptance, openness, and concern for the needs of others. For most participants, the hardest learning is the ability to let other people be as they are, not as the participants would like them to be. The willingness to accept things as they are in the here and now is a primary prerequisite for giving and receiving feedback effectively and for using that feedback for one's own growth.

Norms for giving and asking for feedback must be continuously supported by the training staff, even when the feedback takes place spontaneously in the group (Luft, 1970). Systematic feedback sessions, complemented by the use of instruments, can help to ensure that each member participates and receives some information regarding his or her behavior from everyone in the group. Structured feedback also can be introduced by having members fill out scales describing their reactions to the group in terms of group structure, atmosphere, and cohesion, and in terms of the degree of openness or level of participation of each member.

The Information-Exchange Process

Between two people, the process of feedback exchange is as follows (Figure 1): person A's *intention* is to act in relation to person B, who sees only person A's *behavior*. Between the intention and the behavior is an encoding process that person A uses to ensure that his or her intentions and behavior are congruent. Person B perceives person A's behavior, decodes it (an interpreting process), and intends to respond. Between person B's intention and responding behavior there is also an encoding process. Person A then perceives person B's responding behavior and decodes it.

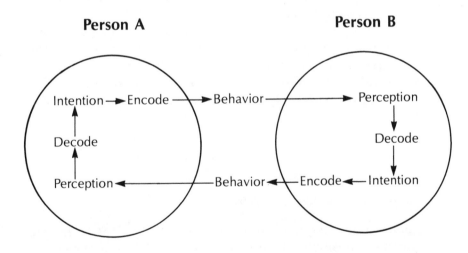

**Figure 1. Giving and Receiving Feedback: A Circular
Communication Process**

If either person's encoding or decoding process is ineffective, the receiver may respond in a manner that will confuse the sender. For example, if one group member's intention is to compliment another by saying, "I really admire Joan's leadership of this group," the first member may be surprised if Joan responds by saying, "I am not leading the group; if I don't talk, no one else will!" Joan's decoding process leads her to hear the message as implying that she is dominating the group. The problem here is that a number of things may have contributed to Joan's response: (a) she may have misread the intention (decoding problem), (b) the sender's statement (behavior) may not have been congruent with his intention (encoding problem), or (c) Joan may actually have read the intention behind the statement correctly, that is, the sender's intention may have been to "put her down" in the guise of a compliment.

Thus, the practice of giving and receiving feedback can help people to discover whether or not their behavior is congruent with their intentions because the process focuses on *behavior* (only they know their intentions). Furthermore, the process highlights the fact that people frequently tend to give feedback about *other* people's intentions, rather than their behavior. By practicing and perfecting one's skill in giving and receiving feedback, one can learn more and more to stay within the here-and-now reality of a situation (the behavior) and can learn to manage the impulse to focus attention on unobservable matters (speculations about intentions, reasons, etc.).

Responsibility for Feedback

The question that frequently arises during feedback exchanges is: how much responsibility should the sender assume for his behavior and the receiver for her response? This question is especially pertinent if the feedback is negative or if it evokes a negative or defensive response. Some people are willing to assume more than their share of responsibility for anything, and other people may refuse to accept any responsibility—even for their own behavior. It is the function of the trainer to guide the group members in exploring their reactions to and utilization of the feedback process. For example, if George is habitually late for the group meetings, he may receive feedback from other members concerning their reactions to his behavior. His response may be to point out to the group members their lack of tolerance for individual differences. He may say that the group members are attempting to limit his freedom and that they seem to be investing too much responsibility in him for the group's effectiveness; he wants to be involved in the group, but does not understand why he needs to be on time.

This situation presents a value dilemma to the group: freedom of choice to change versus pressure to conform. George's observations are accurate, but his behavior is provocative. One way of clarifying this dilemma is to point out that although George is responsible only for his own behavior, the reactions of others inevitably affect him. To the extent that he cares about the others in the group or his relationship with them, he must consider their responses as information to be used in choosing what his interactions with them will be like.

Guidelines for Giving Feedback

It is possible to minimize people's defensiveness about receiving feedback and to maximize their ability to use it for their own personal growth. Feedback must be given in such a way that the person receiving it can *hear* it in the most objective and least distorted way possible, *understand* it, and *choose* to *use* it or *not* to use it. Regardless of how accurate the feedback may be, if individuals cannot accept the information because they are too defensive, the feedback is useless.

The guidelines that follow are listed as if they were bipolar, with the first term in each dimension describing the more effective method of giving feedback.

Direct/Indirect Expression of Feelings

Joe, intending to compliment Marie, says to her, "I wish I could be more selfish, like you." Marie responds, "Why you insensitive boor, what do you mean by saying I'm selfish?" Joe then becomes defensive and retaliates, and the situation rapidly degenerates. Part of the problem here is that Marie hid her hurt feelings behind name-calling. Instead, Marie could have given Joe feedback by stating her feelings directly; that is, she could have said, "When you said you wished you could be more selfish, like me, I felt angry and put down." This method of giving feedback contains positive elements that the first does not. In her initial response, Marie stated her feelings *indirectly*; if she had described them *directly* ("I felt angry and put down"), Joe could have seen clearly what her feelings were and what specific behavior of his ("when you said you wished you could be more selfish like me") triggered these feelings. He might then feel more free to respond positively to her.

If Tom says to Andy, "I like you," he is expressing his feelings directly, risking rejection. However, if he says, "You are a likeable person," the risk is less. Indirect expression of feelings is safer because it is ambiguous and offers an escape from commitment. (If confronted, Tom could deny his own feelings because he has not expressed them directly.) However, it frequently gives only half the message, and the receiver may easily misinterpret the giver's intent.

"You are driving too fast" is an indirect expression of feelings. "I am anxious because you are driving so fast" is a direct expression of feelings. It is obvious that, in the second case, the giver retains responsibility for his or her own feelings rather than attempting to coerce the receiver into assuming the responsibility. It is thus easier for the receiver to hear the message without becoming defensive and cutting off the possibility of acting on the message.

Indirect statements often begin with "I feel that . . ." and finish with a perception, belief, or opinion; for example, "I feel that you are angry." The clue that this type of statement really means "think" and not "feel" is the use of the word "that." "I feel that . . ." almost always means "This is what I really think." "I feel anxious because you look angry" expresses the speaker's feelings directly and also states a perception. The use of the word "feel" is usually authentic when it is followed by a "feeling" (sad, happy, irritated, relieved, etc.). In the workshop setting, participants may need to practice giving and receiving *feeling* messages before they can understand this distinction fully.

Description/Interpretation of Behavior

When Marie says to Joe, "When you said you wished you could be more selfish, like me, I felt angry and put down," Marie is *describing the behavior* to which she is reacting. She is not *attributing a motive* to Joe's behavior, e.g., "You are hostile" or "You do not like me." When one attributes a motive to another person's behavior, one is interpreting that person's *intention*. Since his intention is private and known only to him, any interpretation of his behavior is highly questionable.

In addition, the first person's interpretation may arise from a theory of personality that is not shared by the second person. For example, if William is fidgeting in his chair and shuffling his feet and Walter says, "You are anxious," Walter is interpreting William's behavior. Walter's theory of personality states that when a person fidgets in his chair and shuffles his feet, he is manifesting anxiety. Such a theory interposed between two people can create a barrier between them that precludes understanding. The effectiveness of this barrier can be increased if the receiver's theory conflicts with the giver's. If, instead, Walter *describes* William's behavior, William may then explain his behavior by saying, "My foot is falling asleep."

In any event, interpreting other people's behavior or ascribing motives to it tends to put them on the defensive and cause them to spend their energies on either explaining the behavior or defending themselves. It deprives them of the opportunity to interpret or make sense of their own behavior and may create dependency on the interpreter, particularly if the interpreter is seen as powerful. Such feedback, regardless of how much insight it actually contains, rarely can be used positively.

Nonevaluative/Evaluative Feedback

When giving feedback, one must respond not to the personal worth of the receiver, but to the person's *behavior.* An individual who is told that he is "stupid" or "insensitive" will have great difficulty in responding objectively. A person may sometimes *act* stupidly or *behave* in an insensitive way, but that does not mean that the person is, by nature, stupid or insensitive. In addition to assuming the role of judge, the giver of evaluative feedback assumes that he or she can distinguish categorically between "good" and "bad" or between "right" and "wrong." Such a person may even be surprised when the receiver does not accept the feedback because of the values on which it is based.

It is difficult for people to respond to evaluative feedback because it usually offends their feelings of self-worth or self-esteem. These are core concepts about ourselves that cannot be changed readily by feedback, nor can they be interpreted easily in terms of actual behavior. It is difficult to point out to an individual the specific *behaviors* that manifest many evaluative concepts. If, for example, Joe were to be given feedback that he is "stupid," he probably would not know what *behaviors* he was expected to change. In addition, evaluative feedback frequently engenders defensiveness. When this occurs, the feedback is not likely to be useful or even heard. One way to avoid this is to frame the feedback in terms of the *effect* of the receiver's behavior *on* the sender.

Specific/General Feedback

By describing a *specific* behavior, the giver of feedback tells the receiver to which behavior the giver is reacting. General terms such as "hostile" or "anxious" or "stupid" do not specify *what* evoked the feedback response. Again, the receiver would not know what behavior to change. Even positive feedback expressed in general terms, such as "You are a warm person," does not allow the receiver to know what specific behavior is perceived as warm and, thus, the receiver cannot expand or build on the desired behavior. Again, the complete statement would be something like "When you defended Tom, I felt relieved and grateful to you."

Freedom of Choice/Pressure to Change

If feedback is understood by and important to the receiver, he will probably act on it. If it is not important to him, he may choose not to utilize it. Sometimes an expectation develops in groups that if a member is given feedback he or she *should* act on it, e.g., change the behavior in question. The sequence of feedback and change is not automatic. People should have the freedom to use feedback in any way that is meaningful to them. Imposing standards or demands for change on other people and expecting them to conform arouses resistance and resentment. Such pressures, whether direct or subtle, usually create a win-lose relationship.

Expression of Disappointment As Feedback

Sometimes feedback reflects the sender's disappointment that the receiver did not meet the sender's expectations or hopes. For example, a group leader may be disappointed that some members did not live up to their potential impact on the group or a professor may be disappointed in a student's lack of achievement. These situations represent a dilemma. An important part of the sender's expression of feedback is his or her own feelings, including disappointment or satisfaction. If the sender withholds these feelings, the receiver may be given a false impression. If, however, the sender expresses the disappointment, the receiver may experience the feedback as an indication of personal failure instead of an incentive to change. The sender can resolve part of the dilemma by stating that the feelings and expectations are the sender's *own*, stemming from his or her *own needs*, and that it is not the *responsibility* of the *receiver* to satisfy these feelings or expectations. If the feedback reflects a caring attitude, the receiver may choose to perceive it as encouragement to change.

Persistent Behavior

Frequently, the complaint is heard that some group members persist in behaviors that others find irritating, despite the feedback they receive to that effect. The most the members can do in this case is to continue to confront the offenders with their feelings. In the case of George, for example, although he clearly has the freedom not to change, he also may have to accept the consequences of his decision, i.e., other members' continued irritation about his absences and the likelihood of their punitive reactions. One cannot reasonably expect other group members to feel positive toward one and also to accept a behavior that they find irritating.

Reinforcement of Change

If a member changes a behavior and then does not receive positive feedback regarding the new behavior, the change may not become permanent. However, it is possible that the change may bring about positive or reinforcing consequences other than verbal feedback. For example, as a by-product of change in an individual, other people may change their behavior in relation to that individual. These new responses gradually will become more appropriate to the changed behavior on the part of the first individual.

Immediate/Delayed Timing

To be most effective, feedback should be given immediately after the behavior that prompts it. If time elapses, the receiver may not remember saying or doing the thing in question and other group members may not remember the event. Its significance to other group members may be much less than its significance to the giver of the feedback. When feedback is given immediately after the behavior in question, it acts as a mirror of that behavior, reflecting back to the doer. Also, the event is fresh in everyone's mind and other group members can contribute their observations about the feedback interaction.

Planned Feedback

An exception to the norm of giving immediate feedback is the periodic feedback session, which is planned to keep communication channels open. In these sessions, participants cover events that occurred since the last session or work with material generated during the current meeting. For this process to be effective, however, the decision to have these feedback sessions or to establish a goal for spontaneous feedback should be reached through consensus of the participants.

Group-Shared/External Feedback

When feedback is given immediately after the event, it usually is group shared, so that other members can observe the interaction as it occurs and, perhaps, comment on the appropriateness of its elements. If group members support the sender's feelings and perceptions (consensual validation), the feedback has more potency. If the sender's feedback is not supported by the group members, then the sender would have to look at his or her own behavior and its appropriateness.

Events that occur outside the group (there and then) may be known to only one or two group members and, consequently, cannot be reacted to or discussed meaningfully by other participants, who may feel left out. Because perceptions of outside events are colored by the teller's own biases, these events are not valid material for the other group members to give feedback on. Members may listen empathically to the speakers or ask questions for clarification about the events; but commenting on there-and-then (out of the group) interactions is not the same as giving feedback on events that have occurred in the group.

Use of There-and-Then Material

The relation of there-and-then events to the here and now, and vice versa, can be productive when used as a bridge between the two. It also can be productive if some members have had long-term relationships with one another. It is important, however, to recognize both the necessity and the difficulty of involving other group members in such discussions in meaningful ways.

Consistent Perceptions

Part of each group member's responsibility is to ask for feedback from members who are not responding so the receiver will know how everyone sees his or her behavior. Group members may tend to agree or disagree privately when someone else is giving feedback. The receiver may have to be somewhat aggressive and persistent in seeking this information. Feedback from only one person can present a distorted picture becauase that person's perceptions of the event may differ from those of the other group members. When all members' reactions are given, however, the receiver has a more representative view of his or her behavior from a much broader perspective. If the group members are consistent in their perception of the receiver's behavior, and this disagrees with the receiver's self-perception, then the receiver needs to look more closely at the validity of the self-perception. Even if group members are not in agreement, the fact that people perceive an individual's behavior differently is useful information in itself. When *all* the data have been collected, the receiver is in a better position to make a decision about how to use the feedback.

Solicited/Imposed Feedback

In most exchanges, feedback is imposed. People give feedback whether or not it is solicited and whether or not the other person is prepared to receive it. In addition, the sender's need to give feedback may be much greater than the receiver's need to receive it. This is particularly true when the sender is upset about something concerning the potential recipient. In many situations it is legitimate to impose feedback, particularly when a norm exists for giving as well as for soliciting feedback or in order to induce a norm of spontaneity. However, feedback usually is more helpful when a person solicits it. By asking for feedback, the receiver indicates a willingness to listen and a desire to know how others perceive his or her behavior.

In asking for feedback, it is important to follow some of the same guidelines as in giving feedback. For example, people should be specific about the subjects on which they want feedback. Individuals who say to the group, "I would like the group members to tell me what they think about me" may receive more feedback than they planned. In addition, the request is so general that the group members may be uncertain about where to begin or which behaviors are relevant to the request. In these cases, other group members can help the receiver by asking questions such as "Can you be more specific?" or "About what do you want feedback?" Feedback is a reciprocal process; both senders and receivers can help each other in soliciting and in giving it.

Sometimes is also is important to provide feedback on *how* a person is *giving* feedback. If a receiver is upset, hurt, or angry, other group members can say to the sender, "I, too, feel angry about what you just said to Tom" or "What other way could you have given the relevant information without evaluating or degrading Tom?"

Many people want to know how their behavior is perceived by others but fear the consequences of asking for such information. How easily people will ask for feedback is related to the trust they have in their relationships. One unfortunate consequence of giving feedback is that the receivers may misuse it to reinforce their negative feelings about themselves. This is particularly true of people who have negative self-images. When individuals appear to be using feedback to "put themselves down" or to confirm questionable feelings about their self-esteem, it is helpful to point out what is happening. If this is not done and the process continues, other members eventually may stop giving feedback to the individuals in question because they may begin to feel guilty about "loading it on" those individuals.

Focus on Easy-to-Control/ Difficult-to-Control Behavior

To be effective, feedback should be aimed at behavior that is relatively easy to change. Many individuals' behaviors, however, are habitual and are developed through years of behaving and responding in certain ways. Feedback on these kinds of behaviors is often frustrating because the behaviors may be very difficult to change. Repeated negative feedback about such a behavior (e.g., smoking, biting one's nails) can lead to a sense of failure if the receiver has been unable to change the behavior. In fact, behaviors that serve to reduce tension may be increased as tension builds in the individual as a result of pressure to change.

In giving feedback, one frequently must determine whether or not the behavior in question represents a mere habit or is the result of a deep emotional or other factor. Sometimes it may be helpful to ask whether or not the receiver perceives the behavior to be modifiable. Many behaviors, however, can be changed relatively easily through feedback and the individual's conscious desire to change.

Motivation to Help[1]/Motivation to Hurt

It is assumed that the primary motivation for participation in training is to help oneself and, at the same time, to facilitate the growth of others. When individuals are angry, however, their motives may change to hurting the people toward whom the anger is directed. Frequently, the conflict turns into a win-lose confrontation in which the goal of the interaction is to degrade the other person. It is difficult when one is angry to consider that the needs of the other person are as important as one's own. Feedback that is motivated by anger generally is useless, even when the information is potentially helpful, because the receiver may need to reject the feedback in order to protect his own self-image.

Coping with Anger

There are several ways to cope with anger. One is to engage in a verbal or physical attack; another method is to suppress it. One con-

---

[1]The word "help" as used here means "to help the relationship to be more productive and satisfying." It is not used in the sense of the helper-helpee relationship.

sequence of suppression, however, is that internal pressure builds to the point where one may lose control of one's behavior and act out the feelings destructively. A third, and better, method is to acknowledge and talk about personal feelings of anger without assigning responsibility for them to another person. In this way the anger dissipates without being acted on or suppressed. Anger and conflict are not in themselves "bad"; they are as legitimate as any other feelings. In fact, conflict can be growth producing. It is the manner in which conflict or angry feelings are handled that can have negative consequences. Only through surfacing and resolving conflicts can people develop competence and confidence in dealing with them. Part of the benefit derived from training groups is learning to express anger or to resolve conflicts in constructive, problem-solving ways.

Applying These Guidelines

The process of giving feedback obviously would be hampered if one simultaneously attempted to consider *all* the guidelines given in this chapter. Some are needed more frequently than others, e.g., feedback should be descriptive, nonevaluative, and specific, and should embody freedom of choice; one learns to apply these guidelines through practice.

The preceding guidelines also can be used diagnostically. For example, if the person receiving feedback reacts defensively, some of the guidelines probably have been violated. Group members can ask how the receiver heard the feedback and can help the giver to assess how it was given.

Guidelines for Receiving Feedback

The responsibility for the potential usefulness of feedback lies not only with the giver but also with the receiver. Even though the giver may have utilized all the preceding guidelines, the receiver may still reject, distort, or misunderstand the feedback. There are many people who are not ready or able (for whatever reason) to hear any "criticism" of their behavior without negatively judging themselves or the giver in a way that discourages any further exchange of this kind of information. The problem for the facilitator and other group members is to be sensitive to these issues and, at the same time, to not be manipulated or coerced into supporting the norm of playing it safe or avoiding confrontation. Group members who are extremely anxious about the feedback process can exert considerable pressure, directly or indirectly, on other group members to avoid or dilute their exchanges. A resolution of this issue is to create norms for the exchange of honest feedback and, at the same time, to reinforce norms of encouragement and support rather than for pressure, conformity, or reciprocity. The norms can be facilitated by spelling out ways of receiving feedback that will minimize the tendency to defend against it.

Understanding What Was Said

On receiving feedback, the receiver should make certain that he understands it and should test out his understanding of it with the giver. This may include asking for clarification and amplification and repeating what he heard so that the giver can verify his perception or provide further clarification. The feedback also can be checked with other group members to see if they have the same or different perceptions.

Being Open Rather than Defensive

The recipient of feedback should try to avoid *explaining* the behavior, giving *reasons* or *causes* for it, or immediately rejecting the feedback as invalid. Since the feedback represents another person's experience or reality, it is neither right nor wrong. Immediately rejecting feedback or defending against it shuts off the possibility of adequately understanding other people's perceptions and of examining these perceptions in relation to one's own behavior.

Checking the "Fit"

After checking for understanding and soliciting more than one person's perception, the receiver of feedback should compare the actual behavior in question with the feedback about it. If the feedback "fits," the receiver can decide whether or not to attempt to change the behavior. If the feedback does not fit, it may be rejected or the receiver can decide to keep his options open. The second alternative, of course, is more productive for learning. Once one is alerted to the behaviors referred to in the feedback, one can watch to see if they occur in the future and may even solicit the aid of other members of the group to monitor the behavior in question.

Separating Oneself and One's Behavior

The receiver's attitude is critical to how or whether feedback will be used. If, for example, one experiences the feedback as a threat to one's sense of personal worth or adequacy, the potential benefit of the information may be lost. If the feedback confirms an already negative self-image, it may be misinterpreted or distorted beyond what was actually said. If, on the other hand, one is able to keep one's sense of personal value separate from the behaviors about which one is receiving feedback, the information obtained can have great potential for personal growth. The difference between the *person* and that person's *behavior* may have to be emphasized repeatedly.

The Purposes of Feedback

Each of us has created our own reality concerning others and the world around us. We also participate in another reality "out there" that is reached through agreement. What we see in another individual is a consequence both of what we create and of what we can agree on. Feedback can help to make us more aware of ourselves by showing us how we are experienced from another individual's unique point of view and from the group's point of view. One person's experience of another is important in order to clarify the relationship between them, even if one's experience of the other is quite different from the group's experience of that person. One provides a unique experience, the other a social reality. Giving and receiving feedback, therefore, may serve several purposes:

1. Feedback from others helps us to be aware of their experience of us. It is a way of monitoring or checking out how the relationship is going in the eyes of the other person or group.

2. Feedback enables us to know how we are progressing toward our goals. It can act as a corrective steering device when we deviate from the path toward our goals and can guide subsequent behavior in the desired direction.

3. Feedback enables us to know the effect of our behavior on others. It validates or invalidates our intentions in terms of what we actually do or say. That is, feedback serves as a check on reality.

4. Feedback enables us to compare our self-perceptions with the perceptions of others and help us to see ourselves as others do.

5. The process of giving and receiving feedback teaches us to be more observant about our own and others' behaviors and to distinguish, more accurately, what we observe from what we attribute.

6. As the norm for exchanging feedback develops in the group, a standard of objectivity also is established. Feedback about behavior is seen as information to be examined as any other kind of information would be.

References

Lewin, K. (1947). Frontiers in group dynamics: I. Concept, method and reality in social science: Social equilibria and social change. *Human Relations, 1*(1), 5-41.

Lewin, K. (1951). *Field theory in social science: Selected Papers.* (D. Cartwright, Ed.). New York: Harper & Row.

Luft, J. (1970). *Group processes: An introduction to group dynamics* (2nd ed.). Palo Alto, CA: Mayfield.